JEFF BRIGGS'S LOVE STORY

BRET HARTE

1st WORLD
LIBRARY
Literary Society

Jeff Briggs's Love Story

Bret Harte

© 1st World Library, 2007
PO Box 2211
Fairfield, IA 52556
www.1stworldlibrary.com
First Edition

LCCN: 2007934099

Softcover ISBN: 978-1-4218-9625-0
Hardcover ISBN: 978-1-4218-9725-7
eBook ISBN: 978-1-4218-9525-3

Purchase *"Jeff Briggs's Love Story"*
as a traditional bound book at:
www.1stWorldLibrary.com/purchase.asp?ISBN=978-1-4218-9625-0

1st World Library is a literary, educational organization
dedicated to:

- Creating a free internet library of downloadable ebooks

- Hosting writing competitions and offering book publishing
  scholarships.

Interested in more 1st World Library books? contact:
literacy@1stworldlibrary.com
Check us out at: www.1stworldlibrary.com

1ˢᵗ World Library Literary Society

Giving Back to the World

"If you want to work on the core problem, it's early school literacy."

- James Barksdale, former CEO of Netscape

"No skill is more crucial to the future of a child, or to a democratic and prosperous society, than literacy."

- Los Angeles Times

"Literacy... means far more than learning how to read and write... The aim is to transmit... knowledge and promote social participation."

- UNESCO

"Literacy is not a luxury, it is a right and a responsibility. If our world is to meet the challenges of the twenty-first century we must harness the energy and creativity of all our citizens."

- President Bill Clinton

"Parents should be encouraged to read to their children, and teachers should be equipped with all available techniques for teaching literacy, so the varying needs and capacities of individual kids can be taken into account."

- Hugh Mackay

I

It was raining and blowing at Eldridge's Crossing. From the stately pine-trees on the hill-tops, which were dignifiedly protesting through their rigid spines upward, to the hysterical willows in the hollow, that had whipped themselves into a maudlin fury, there was a general tumult. When the wind lulled, the rain kept up the distraction, firing long volleys across the road, letting loose miniature cataracts from the hill-sides to brawl in the ditches, and beating down the heavy heads of wild oats on the levels; when the rain ceased for a moment the wind charged over the already defeated field, ruffled the gullies, scattered the spray from the roadside pines, and added insult to injury. But both wind and rain concentrated their energies in a malevolent attempt to utterly disperse and scatter the "Half-way House," which seemed to have wholly lost its way, and strayed into the open, where, dazed and bewildered, unprepared and unprotected, it was exposed to the taunting fury of the blast. A loose, shambling, disjointed, hastily built structure—representing the worst features of Pioneer renaissance—it rattled its loose window-sashes like chattering teeth, banged its ill-hung shutters, and admitted so much of the invading storm, that it might have blown up or blown down with equal facility.

Jefferson Briggs, proprietor and landlord of the "Half-way House," had just gone through the formality of closing his house for the night, hanging dangerously out of the window in the vain attempt to subdue a rebellious shutter that had evidently entered into conspiracy with the invaders, and, shutting a door as against a sheriff's posse, was going to bed—i. e., to read himself asleep, as was his custom. As he entered his little bedroom in the attic with a highly exciting novel in his pocket and a kerosene lamp in his hand, the wind, lying in wait for him, instantly extinguished his lamp and slammed the door behind him. Jefferson Briggs relighted the lamp, as if confidentially, in a corner, and, shielding it in the bosom of his red flannel shirt, which gave him the appearance of an illuminated shrine, hung a heavy bear-skin across the window, and then carefully deposited his lamp upon a chair at his bedside. This done, he kicked off his boots, flung them into a corner, and, rolling himself in a blanket, lay down upon the bed. A habit of early rising, bringing with it, presumably, the proverbial accompaniment of health, wisdom, and pecuniary emoluments, had also brought with it certain ideas of the effeminacy of separate toilettes and the virtue of readiness.

In a few moments he was deep in a chapter.

A vague pecking at his door—as of an unseasonable wood-pecker, finally asserted itself to his consciousness. "Come in," he said, with his eye still on the page.

The door opened to a gaunt figure, partly composed of bed-quilt and partly of plaid shawl. A predominance of the latter and a long wisp of iron-gray hair determined her sex. She leaned against the post with an air of fatigue, half moral and half physical.

"How ye kin lie thar, abed, Jeff, and read and smoke on sich a night! The sperrit o' the Lord abroad over the yearth—and up stage not gone by yet. Well, well! it's well thar ez SOME

EZ CAN'T SLEEP."

"The up coach, like ɛs rot, is stopped by high water on the North Fork, ten miles away, aunty," responded Jeff, keeping to the facts. Possibly not recognizing the hand of the beneficent Creator in the rebellious window shutter, he avoided theology.

"Well," responded the figure, with an air of delivering an unheeded and thankless warning, "it is not for ME to say. P'raps it's all His wisdom that some will keep to their own mind. It's well ez some hezn't narves, and kin luxuriate in terbacker in the night watches. But He says, 'I'll come like a thief in the night!'—like a thief in the night, Jeff."

Totally unable to reconcile this illustration with the delayed "Pioneer" coach and Yuba Bill, its driver, Jeff lay silent. In his own way, perhaps, he was uneasy—not to say shocked— at his aunt's habitual freedom of scriptural quotation, as that good lady herself was with an occasional oath from his lips; a fact, by the way, nct generally understood by purveyors of Scripture, licensed and unlicensed.

"I'd take a pull at them bitters, aunty," said Jeff feebly, with his wandering eye still recurring to his page. "They'll do ye a power of good in the way o' calmin' yer narves."

"Ef I was like some folks I wouldn't want bitters—though made outer the simplest yarbs of the yearth, with jest enough sperrit to bring out the vartoos—ez Deacon Stoer's Balm 'er Gilead is—what yer meaning? Ef I was like some folks I could lie thar and smoke in the lap o' idleness—with fourteen beds in the house empty, and nary lodger for one of 'em. Ef I was that indifferent to havin' invested my fortin in the good will o' this house, and not ez much ez a single transient lookin' in, I could lie down and take comfort in profane literatoor. But it ain't in me to do it. And it wasn't your father's way, Jeff, neither!"

As the elder Briggs's way had been to seek surcease from such trouble at the gambling table, and eventually, in suicide, Jeff could not deny it. But he did not say that a full realization of his unhappy venture overcame him as he closed the blinds of the hotel that night; and that the half desperate idea of abandoning it then and there to the warring elements that had resented his trespass on Nature seemed to him an act of simple reason and justice. He did not say this, for easy-going natures are not apt to explain the processes by which their content or resignation is reached, and are therefore supposed to have none. Keeping to the facts, he simply suggested the weather was unfavorable to travelers, and again found his place on the page before him. Fixing it with his thumb, he looked up resignedly. The figure wearily detached itself from the door-post, and Jeff's eyes fell on his book. "You won't stop, aunty?" he asked mechanically, as if reading aloud from the page; but she was gone.

A little ashamed, although much relieved, Jeff fell back again to literature, interrupted only by the charging of the wind and the heavy volleys of rain. Presently he found himself wondering if a certain banging were really a shutter, and then, having settled in his mind that it WAS, he was startled by a shout. Another, and in the road before the house!

Jeff put down the book, and marked the place by turning down the leaf, being one of that large class of readers whose mental faculties are butter-fingered, and easily slip their hold. Then he resumed his boots and was duly caparisoned. He extinguished the kerosene lamp, and braved the outer air, and strong currents of the hall and stairway in the darkness. Lighting two candles in the bar-room, he proceeded to unlock the hall door. At the same instant a furious blast shook the house, the door yielded slightly and impelled a thin, meek-looking stranger violently against Jeff, who still struggled with it.

"An accident has occurred," began the stranger, "and"—but here the wind charged again, blew open the door, pinned Jeff behind it back against the wall, overturned the dripping stranger, dashed up the staircase, and slammed every door in the house, ending triumphantly with No. 14, and a crash of glass in the window.

"'Come, rouse up!" said Jeff, still struggling with the door, "rouse up and lend a hand yer!"

Thus abjured, the stranger crept along the wall towards Jeff and began again, "We have met with an accident." But here another and mightier gust left him speechless, covered him with spray of a wildly disorganized water-spout that, dangling from the roof, seemed to be playing on the front door, drove him into black obscurity and again sandwiched his host between the door and the wall. Then there was a lull, and in the midst of it Yuba Bill, driver of the "Pioneer" coach, quietly and coolly, impervious in waterproof, walked into the hall, entered the bar-room, took a candle, and, going behind the bar, selected a bottle, critically examined it, and, returning, poured out a quantity of whiskey in a glass and gulped it in a single draught.

All this while Jeff was closing the door, and the meek-looking man was coming into the light again.

Yuba Bill squared his elbows behind him and rested them on the bar, crossed his legs easily and awaited them. In reply to Jeff's inquiring but respectful look, he said shortly—

"Oh, you're thar, are ye?"

"Yes, Bill."

"Well, this yer new-fangled road o' yours is ten feet deep in the hollow with back water from the North Fork! I've taken that yar coach inter fower feet of it, and then I reckoned I couldn't hev any more. 'I'll stand on this yer hand,' sez I; I brought the horses up yer and landed 'em in your barn to eat their blessed heads off till the water goes down. That's wot's the matter, old man, and jist about wot I kalkilated on from those durned old improvements o' yours."

Coloring a little at this new count in the general indictment against the uselessness of the "Half-way House," Jeff asked if there were "any passengers?"

Yuba Bill indicated the meek stranger with a jerk of his thumb. "And his wife and darter in the coach. They're all right and tight, ez if they was in the Fifth Avenue Hotel. But I reckon he allows to fetch 'em up yer," added Bill, as if he strongly doubted the wisdom of the transfer.

The meek man, much meeker for the presence of Bill, here suggested that such indeed was his wish, and further prayed that Jeff would accompany him to the coach to assist in bringing them up. "It's rather wet and dark," said the man apologetically; "my daughter is not strong. Have you such a thing as a waterproof?"

Jeff had not; but would a bear-skin do?

It would.

Jeff ran, tore down his extempore window curtain, and returned with it. Yuba Bill, who had quietly and disapprovingly surveyed the proceeding, here disengaged himself from the bar with evident reluctance.

"You'll want another man," he said to Jeff, "onless ye can carry double. Ez HE," indicating the stranger, "ez no sort o' use, he'd better stay here and 'tend bar,' while you and me fetch the wimmen off. 'Specially ez I reckon we've got to do some tall wadin' by this time to reach 'em."

The meek man sat down helplessly in a chair indicated by Bill, who at once strode after Jeff. In another moment they were both fighting their way, step by step, against the storm, in that peculiar, drunken, spasmodic way so amusing to the spectator and so exasperating to the performer. It was no time for conversation, even interjectional profanity was dangerously exhaustive.

The coach was scarcely a thousand yards away, but its bright lights were reflected in a sheet of dark silent water that stretched between it and the two men. Wading and splashing, they soon reached it, and a gully where the surplus water was pouring into the valley below. "Fower feet o' water round her, but can't get any higher. So ye see she's all right for a month o' sich weather." Inwardly admiring the perspicacity of his companion, Jeff was about to open the coach door when Bill interrupted.

"I'll pack the old woman, if you'll look arter the darter and enny little traps."

A female face, anxious and elderly, here appeared at the window.

"Thet's my little game," said Bill, sotto voce.

"Is there any danger? where is my husband?" asked the

woman impatiently.

"Ez to the danger, ma'am,—thar ain't any. Yer ez safe HERE ez ye'd be in a Sacramento steamer; ez to your husband, he allowed I was to come yer and fetch yer up to the hotel. That's his look-out!" With this cheering speech, Bill procee-ded to make two or three ineffectual scoops into the dark interior, manifestly with the idea of scooping out the lady in question. In another instant he had caught her, lifted her gently but firmly in his arms, and was turning away.

"But my child!—my daughter! she's asleep!"—expostulated the woman; but Bill was already swiftly splashing through the darkness. Jeff, left to himself, hastily examined the coach: on the back seat a slight small figure, enveloped in a shawl, lay motionless. Jeff threw the bear-skin over it gently, lifted it on one arm, and gathering a few travelling bags and baskets with the other, prepared to follow his quickly disappearing leader. A few feet from the coach the water appeared to deepen, and the bear-skin to draggle. Jeff drew the figure up higher, in vain.

"Sis," he said softly.

No reply.

"Sis," shaking her gently.

There was a slight movement within the wrappings.

"Couldn't ye climb up on my shoulder, honey? that's a good child!"

There were one or two spasmodic jerks of the bear-skin, and, aided by Jeff, the bundle was presently seated on his shoulder.

"Are you all right now, Sis?"

Something like a laugh came from the bear-skin. Then a childish voice said, "Thank you, I think I am!"

"Ain't you afraid you'll fall off?"

"A little."

Jeff hesitated. It was beginning to blow again.

"You couldn't reach down and put your arm round my neck, could ye, honey?"

"I am afraid not!"—although there WAS a slight attempt to do so.

"No?"

"No!"

"Well, then, take a good holt, a firm strong holt, o' my hair! Don't be afraid!"

A small hand timidly began to rummage in Jeff's thick curls.

"Take a firm holt; thar, just back o' my neck! That's right."

The little hand closed over half a dozen curls. The little figure shook, and giggled.

"Now don't you see, honey, if I'm keerless with you, and don't keep you plump level up thar, you jist give me a pull and fetch me up all standing!"

"I see!"

"Of course you do! That's because you're a little lady!"

Jeff strode on. It was pleasant to feel the soft warm fingers in his hair, pleasant to hear the faint childish voice, pleasant to draw the feet of the enwrapped figure against his broad breast. Altogether he was sorry when they reached the dry land and the lee of the "Half-way House," where a slight movement of the figure expressed a wish to dismount.

"Not yet, missy," said Jeff; "not yet! You'll get blown away, sure! And then what'll they say? No, honey! I'll take you right in to your papa, just as ye are!"

A few steps more and Jeff strode into the hall, made his way to the sitting-room, walked to the sofa, and deposited his burden. The bear-skin fell back, the shawl fell back, and Jeff—fell back too! For before him lay a small, slight, but beautiful and perfectly formed woman.

He had time to see that the meek man, no longer meek, but apparently a stern uncompromising parent, was standing at the head of the sofa; that the elderly and nervous female was hovering at the foot, that his aunt, with every symptom of religious and moral disapproval of his conduct, sat rigidly in one of the rigid chairs—he had time to see all this before the quick, hot blood, flying to his face, sent the water into his eyes, and he could see nothing!

The cause of all this smiled—a dazzling smile though a faint one—that momentarily lit up the austere gloom of the room and its occupants. "You must thank this gentleman, papa," said she, languidly turning to her father, "for his kindness and his trouble. He has carried me here as gently and as carefully as if I were a child." Seeing symptoms of a return of Jeff's distress in his coloring face, she added softly, as if to herself, "It's a great thing to be strong—a greater thing to be strong AND gentle."

The voice thrilled through Jeff. But into this dangerous human voice twanged the accents of special spiritual revelation, and called him to himself again, "Be ye wise as sarpints, but harmless as duvs," said Jeff's aunt, generally, "and let 'em be thankful ez doesn't aboos the stren'th the Lord gives 'em, but be allers ready to answer for it at the bar c' their Maker." Possibly some suggestion in her figure of speech reminded her of Jeff's forgotten duties, so she added in the same breath and tone, "especially when transient customers is waiting for their licker, and Yuba Bill hammerin' on the counter with his glass; and yer ye stand, Jeff, never even takin' up that wet bar-skin—enuff to give that young woman her death."

Stammering out an incoherent apology, addressed vaguely to the occupants of the room, but looking toward the languid goddess on the sofa, Jeff seized the bear-skin and backed out the door. Then he flew to his room with it, and then returned to the bar-room; but the impatient William of Yuba had characteristically helped himself and gone off to the stable. Then Jeff stole into the hall and halted before the closed door of the sitting-room. A bold idea of going in again, as became a landlord of the "Half-way House," with an inquiry if they wished anything further, had seized him, but the remembrance that he had always meekly allowed that duty to devolve upon his aunt, and that she would probably resent it with scriptural authority and bring him to shame again, stayed his timid knuckles at the door. In this hesitation he stumbled upon his aunt coming down the stairs with an armful of blankets and pillows, attended by their small Indian servant, staggering under a mattress.

"Is everything all right, aunty?"

"Ye kin be thankful to the Lord, Jeff Briggs, that this didn't happen last week when I was down on my back with rheumatiz. But ye're never grateful."

"The young lady—is SHE comfortable?" said Jeff, accepting his aunt's previous remark as confirmatory.

"Ez well ez enny critter marked by the finger of the Lord with gallopin' consumption kin be, I reckon. And she, ez oughter be putting off airthly vanities, askin' for a lookin'-glass! And you! trapesin' through the hall with her on yer shoulder, and dancin' and jouncin' her up and down ez if it was a ball-room!" A guilty recollection that he had skipped with her through the passage struck him with remorse as his aunt went on: "It's a mercy that betwixt you and the wet bar-skin she ain't got her deth!"

"Don't ye think, aunty," stammered Jeff, "that—that—my bein' the landlord, yer know, it would be the square thing—just out o' respect, ye know—for me to drop in thar and ask 'em if thar's anythin' they wanted?"

His aunt stopped, and resignedly put down the pillows. "Sarah," she said meekly to the handmaiden, "ye kin leave go that mattress. Yer's Mr. Jefferson thinks we ain't good enough to make the beds for them two city women folks, and he allows he'll do it himself!"

"No, no! aunty!" began the horrified Jeff; but failing to placate his injured relative, took safety in flight.

Once safe in his own room his eye fell on the bear-skin. It certainly WAS wet. Perhaps he had been careless—perhaps he had imperiled her life! His cheeks flushed as he threw it hastily in the corner. Something fell from it to the floor. Jeff picked it up and held it to the light. It was a small, a very

Bret Harte

small, lady's slipper. Holding it within the palm of his hand as if it had been some delicate flower which the pressure of a finger might crush, he strode to the door, but stopped. Should he give it to his aunt? Even if she overlooked this evident proof of HIS carelessness, what would she think of the young lady's? Ought he—seductive thought!—go downstairs again, knock at the door, and give it to its fair owner, with the apology he was longing to make? Then he remembered that he had but a few moments before been dismissed from the room very much as if he were the original proprietor of the skin he had taken. Perhaps they were right; perhaps he WAS only a foolish clumsy animal! Yet SHE had thanked him—and had said in her sweet childlike voice, "It is a great thing to be strong; a greater thing to be strong and gentle." He was strong; strong men had said so. He did not know if he was gentle too. Had she meant THAT, when she turned her strangely soft dark eyes upon him? For some moments he held the slipper hesitatingly in his hand, then he opened his trunk, and disposing various articles around it as if it were some fragile, perishable object, laid it carefully therein.

This done, he drew off his boots, and rolling himself in his blanket, lay down upon the bed. He did not open his novel— he did not follow up the exciting love episode of his favorite hero—so ungrateful is humanity to us poor romancers, in the first stages of their real passion. Ah, me! 'tis the jongleurs and troubadours they want then, not us! When Master Slender, sick for sweet Anne Page, would "rather than forty shillings" he had his "book of songs and sonnets" there, what availed it that the Italian Boccaccio had contemporaneously discoursed wisely and sweetly of love in prose? I doubt not that Master Jeff would have mumbled some verse to himself had he known any: knowing none, he lay there and listened to the wind.

Did she hear it; did it keep her awake? He had an uneasy

suspicion that the shutter that was banging so outrageously was the shutter of her room. Filled with this miserable thought, he arose softly, stole down the staircase, and listened. The sound was repeated. It was truly the refractory shutter of No. 7—the best bedroom adjoining the sitting-room. The next room, No. 8, was vacant. Jeff entered it softly, as softly opened the window, and leaning far out in the tempest, essayed to secure the nocturnal disturber. But in vain. Cord or rope he had none, nor could he procure either without alarming his aunt—an extremity not to be considered. Jeff was a man of clumsy but forceful expedients. He hung far out of the window, and with one powerful hand lifted the shutter off its hinges and dragged it softly into No. 8. Then as softly he crept upstairs to bed. The wind howled and tore round the house; the crazy water-pipe below Jeff's window creaked, the chimneys whistled, but the shutter banged no more. Jeff began to doze. "It's a great thing to be strong," the wind seemed to say as it charged upon the defenseless house, and then another voice seemed to reply, "A greater thing to be strong and gentle;" and hearing this he fell asleep.

Bret Harte

II

It was not yet daylight when he awoke with an idea that brought him hurriedly to his feet. Quickly dressing himself, he began to count the money in his pocket. Apparently the total was not satisfactory, as he endeavored to augment it by loose coins fished from the pockets of his other garments, and from the corner of his washstand drawer. Then he cautiously crept downstairs, seized his gun, and stole out of the still sleeping house. The wind had gone down, the rain had ceased, a few stars shone steadily in the north, and the shapeless bulk of the coach, its lamps extinguished, loomed high and dry above the lessening water, in the twilight. With a swinging tread Jeff strode up the hill and was soon upon the highway and stage road. A half-hour's brisk walk brought him to the summit, and the first rosy flashes of morning light. This enabled him to knock over half-a-dozen early quail, lured by the proverb, who were seeking their breakfast in the chaparral, and gave him courage to continue on his mission, which his perplexed face and irresolute manner had for the last few moments shown to be an embarrassing one. At last the white fences and imposing outbuildings of the "Summit Hotel" rose before him, and he uttered a deep sigh. There, basking in the first rays of the morning sun, stood his successful rival! Jeff looked at the well-built, comfortable structure, the commanding site, and the air of serene independence that seemed to possess it, and no longer wondered that the great world passed him by to linger and refresh itself there.

He was relieved to find the landlord was not present in person, and so confided his business to the bar-keeper. At first it appeared that that functionary declined interference, and with many head-shakings and audible misgivings was inclined to await the coming of his principal, but a nearer view of Jeff's perplexed face, and an examination of Jeff's gun, and the few coins spread before him, finally induced him to produce certain articles, which he packed in a basket and handed to Jeff, taking the gun and coins in exchange. Thus relieved, Jeff set his face homewards, and ran a race with the morning into the valley, reaching the "Half-way House" as the sun laid waste its bare, bleak outlines, and relentlessly pointed out its defects one by one. It was cruel to Jeff at that moment, but he hugged his basket close and slipped to the back door and the kitchen, where his aunt was already at work.

"I didn't know ye were up yet, aunty," said Jeff submissively. "It isn't more than six o'clock."

"Thar's four more to feed at breakfast," said his aunt severely, "and yer's the top blown off the kitchen chimbly, and the fire only just got to go."

Jeff saw that he was in time. The ordinary breakfast of the "Half-way House," not yet prepared, consisted of codfish, ham, yellow-ochre biscuit, made after a peculiar receipt of his aunt's, and potatoes.

"I got a few fancy fixin's up at the Summit this morning, aunty," he began apologetically, "seein' we had sick folks, you know—you and the young lady—and thinkin' it might save you trouble. I've got 'em here," and he shyly produced the basket.

"If ye kin afford it, Jeff," responded his aunt resignedly, "I'm thankful."

The reply was so unexpectedly mild for Aunt Sally, that Jeff put his arms around her and kissed her hard cheek. "And I've got some quail, aunty, knowin' you liked em."

"I reckoned you was up to some such foolishness," said Aunt Sally, wiping her cheek with her apron, "when I missed yer gun from the hall." But the allusion was a dangerous one, and Jeff slipped away.

He breakfasted early with Yuba Bill that morning; the latter gentleman's taciturnity being intensified at such moments through a long habit of confining himself strictly to eating in the limited time allowed his daily repasts, and it was not until they had taken the horses from the stable and were harnessing them to the coach that Jeff extracted from his companion some facts about his guests. They were Mr. and Mrs. Mayfield, Eastern tourists, who had been to the Sandwich Islands for the benefit of their daughter's health, and before returning to New York, intended, under the advice of their physician, to further try the effects of mountain air at the "Summit Hotel," on the invalid. They were apparently rich people, the coach had been engaged for them solely—even the mail and express had been sent on by a separate conveyance, so that they might be more independent. It is hardly necessary to say that this fact was by no means palatable to Bill—debarring him not only the social contact and attentions of the "Express Agent," but the selection of a box-seated passenger who always "acted like a man."

"Ye kin kalkilate what kind of a pardner that 'ar yaller-livered

Mayfield would make up on that box, partik'ly ez I heard before we started that he'd requested the kimpany's agent in Sacramento to select a driver ez didn't cuss, smoke, or drink. He did, sir, by gum!"

"I reckon you were very careful, then, Bill," said Jeff.

"In course," returned Bill, with a perfectly diabolical wink. "In course! You know that 'Blue Grass,'" pointing out a spirited leader; "she's a fair horse ez horses go, but she's apt to feel her oats on a down grade, and takes a pow'ful deal o' soothin' and explanation afore she buckles down to her reg'lar work. Well, sir, I exhorted and labored in a Christian-like way with that mare to that extent that I'm cussed if that chap didn't want to get down afore we got to the level!"

"And the ladies?" asked Jeff, whose laugh—possibly from his morning's experience—was not as ready as formerly.

"The ladies! Ef you mean that 'ar livin' skellington I packed up to yer house," said Bill promptly, "it's a pair of them in size and color, and ready for any first-class undertaker's team in the kintry. Why, you remember that curve on Break Neck hill, where the leaders allus look as if they was alongside o' the coach and faced the other way? Well, that woman sticks her skull outer the window, and sez she, confidential-like to old yaller-belly, sez she, 'William Henry,' sez she, 'tell that man his horses are running away!'"

"You didn't get to see the—the—daughter, Bill, did you?" asked Jeff, whose laugh had become quite uneasy.

"No, I didn't," said Bill, with sudden and inexplicable vehemence, "and the less you see of her, Jefferson Briggs, the better for you."

Too confounded and confused by Bill's manner to question further, Jeff remained silent until they drew up at the door of the "Half-way House." But here another surprise awaited him. Mr. Mayfield, erect and dignified, stood upon the front porch as the coach drove up.

"Driver!" began Mr. Mayfield.

There was no reply.

"Driver," said Mr. Mayfield, slightly weakening under Bill's eye, "I shall want you no longer. I have"—

"Is he speaking to me?" said Bill audibly to Jeff, "'cause they call me 'Yuba Bill' yer abouts."

"He is," said Jeff hastily.

"Mebbee he's drunk," said Bill audibly; "a drop or two afore breakfast sometimes upsets his kind."

"I was saying, Bill," said Mr. Mayfield, becoming utterly limp and weak again under Bill's cold gray eyes, "that I've changed my mind, and shall stop here awhile. My daughter seems already benefited by the change. You can take my traps from the boot and leave them here."

Bill laid down his lines resignedly, coolly surveyed Mr. Mayfield, the house, and the half-pleased, half-frightened Jeff, and then proceeded to remove the luggage from the boot, all the while whistling loud and offensive incredulity. Then he climbed back to his box. Mr. Mayfield, completely demoralized under this treatment, as a last resort essayed patronage.

"You can say to the Sacramento agents, Bill, that I am

entirely satisfied, and"—

"Ye needn't fear but I'll give ye a good character," interrupted Bill coolly, gathering up his lines. The whip snapped, the six horses dashed forward as one, the coach plunged down the road and was gone.

With its disappearance, Mr. Mayfield stiffened slightly again. "I have just told your aunt, Mr. Briggs," he said, turning upon Jeff, "that my daughter has expressed a desire to remain here a few days; she has slept well, seems to be invigorated by the air, and although we expected to go on to the 'Summit,' Mrs. Mayfield and myself are willing to accede to her wishes. Your house seems to be new and clean. Your table—judging from the breakfast this morning—is quite satisfactory."

Jeff, in the first flush of delight at this news, forgot what that breakfast had cost him—forgot all his morning's experience, and, I fear, when he did remember it, was too full of a vague, hopeful courage to appreciate it. Conscious of showing too much pleasure, he affected the necessity of an immediate interview with his aunt, in the kitchen. But his short cut round the house was arrested by a voice and figure. It was Miss Mayfield, wrapped in a shawl and seated in a chair, basking in the sunlight at one of the bleakest and barest angles of the house. Jeff stopped in a delicious tremor.

As we are dealing with facts, however, it would be well to look at the cause of this tremor with our own eyes and not Jeff's. To be plain, my dear madam, as she basked in that remorseless, matter-of-fact California sunshine, she looked her full age-twenty-five, if a day! There were wrinkles in the corners of her dark eyes, contracted and frowning in that strong, merciless light; there was a nervous pallor in her complexion; but being one of those "fast colored" brunettes, whose dyes are a part of their temperament, no sickness nor wear could bleach it out. The red of her small mouth was darker than yours, I wot, and there were certain faint lines from the corners of her delicate nostrils indicating alternate repression and excitement under certain experiences, which are not found in the classic ideals. Now Jeff knew nothing of the classic ideal—did not know that a thousand years ago certain sensual idiots had, with brush and chisel, inflicted upon the world the personification of the strongest and most delicate, most controlling and most subtle passion that humanity is capable of, in the likeness of a thick-waisted, idealess, expressionless, perfectly contented female animal; and that thousands of idiots had since then insisted upon perpetuating this model for the benefit of a world that had gone on sighing for, pining for, fighting for, and occasionally blowing its brains out over types far removed from that idiotic standard.

Consequently Jeff saw only a face full of possibilities and probabilities, framed in a small delicate oval, saw a slight woman's form—more than usually small—and heard a low voice, to him full of gentle pride, passion, pathos, and human weakness, and was helpless.

"I only said 'Good-morning,'" said Miss Mayfield, with that slight, arch satisfaction in the observation of masculine bashfulness, which the best of her sex cannot forego.

"Thank you, miss; good-morning. I've been wanting to say to you that I hope you wasn't mad, you know," stammered Jeff, desperately intent upon getting off his apology.

"It is so lovely this morning—such a change!" continued Miss Mayfield.

"Yes, miss! You know I reckoned—at least what your father

said, made me kalkilate that you"—

Miss Mayfield, still smiling, knitted her brows and went on: "I slept so well last night," she said gratefully, "and feel so much better this morning, that I ventured out. I seem to be drinking in health in this clear sunlight."

"Certainly miss. As I was sayin', your father says his daughter is in the coach; and Bill says, says he to me, 'I'll pack—I'll carry the old—I'll bring up Mrs. Mayfield, if you'll bring up the daughter;' and when we come to the coach I saw you asleep—like in the corner, and bein' small, why miss, you know how nat'ral it is, I"—

"Oh, Mr. Jeff! Mr. Briggs!" said Miss Mayfield plaintively, "don't, please—don't spoil the best compliment I've had in many a year. You thought I was a child, I know, and—well, you find," she said audaciously, suddenly bringing her black eyes to bear on him like a rifle, "you find—well?"

What Jeff thought was inaudible but not invisible. Miss Mayfield saw enough of it in his eye to protest with a faint color in her cheek. Thus does Nature betray itself to Nature the world over.

The color faded. "It's a dreadful thing to be so weak and helpless, and to put everybody to such trouble, isn't it, Mr. Jeff? I beg your pardon—your aunt calls you Jeff."

"Please call me Jeff," said Jeff, to his own surprise rapidly gaining courage. "Everybody calls me that."

Miss Mayfield smiled. "I suppose I must do what everybody does. So it seems that we are to give you the trouble of keeping us here until I get better or worse?"

"Yes, miss."

"Therefore I won't detain you now. I only wanted to thank you for your gentleness last night, and to assure you that the bear-skin did not give me my death."

She smiled and nodded her small head, and wrapped her shawl again closely around her shoulders, and turned her eyes upon the mountains, gestures which the now quick-minded Jeff interpreted as a gentle dismissal, and flew to seek his aunt.

Here he grew practical. Ready money was needed; for the "Half-way House" was such a public monument of ill-luck, that Jeff had no credit. He must keep up the table to the level of that fortunate breakfast—to do which he had $1.50 in the till, left by Bill, and $2.50 produced by his Aunt Sally from her work-basket.

"Why not ask Mr. Mayfield to advance ye suthin?" said Aunt Sally.

The blood flew to Jeff's face. "Never! Don't say that again, aunty."

The tone and manner were so unlike Jeff that the old lady sat down half frightened, and taking the corners of her apron in her hands began to whimper.

"Thar now, aunty! I didn't mean nothin',—only if you care to have me about the place any longer, and I reckon it's little good I am any way," he added, with a new-found bitterness in his tone, "ye'll not ask me to do that."

"What's gone o' ye, Jeff?" said his aunt lugubriously; "ye ain't nat'ral like."

Jeff laughed. "See here, aunty; I'm goin' to take your advice. You know Rabbit?"

"The mare?"

"Yes; I'm going to sell her. The blacksmith offered me a hundred dollars for her last week."

"Ef ye'd done that a month ago, Jeff, ez I wanted ye to, instead o' keeping the brute to eat ye out o' house and home, ye'd be better off." Aunt Sally never let slip an opportunity to "improve the occasion," but preferred to exhort over the prostrate body of the "improved." "Well, I hope he mayn't change his mind."

Jeff smiled at such suggestion regarding the best horse within fifty miles of the "Half-way House." Nevertheless he went briskly to the stable, led out and saddled a handsome grey mare, petting her the while, and keeping up a running commentary of caressing epithets to which Rabbit responded with a whinny and playful reaches after Jeff's red flannel sleeve. Whereat Jeff, having loved the horse until it was displaced by another mistress, grew grave and suddenly threw his arms around Rabbit's neck, and then taking Rabbit's nose, thrust it in the bosom of his shirt and held it there silently for a moment. Rabbit becoming uneasy, Jeff's mood changed too, and having caparisoned himself and charger in true vaquero style, not without a little Mexican dandyism as to the set of his doeskin trousers, and the tie of his red sash, put a sombrero rakishly on his curls and leaped into the saddle.

Jeff was a fair rider in a country where riding was understood as a natural instinct, and not as a purely artificial habit of horse and rider, consequently he was not perched up, jockey fashion, with a knee-grip for his body, and a rein-rest for his arms on the beast's mouth, but rode with long, loose stirrups, his legs clasping the barrel of his horse, his single rein lying loose upon her neck, leaving her head free as the wind. After this fashion he had often emerged from a cloud of dust on the red mountain road, striking admiration into the hearts of the wayfarers and coach-passengers, and leaving a trail of pleasant incense in the dust behind him. It was therefore with considerable confidence in himself, and a little human vanity, that he dashed round the house, and threw his mare skilfully on her haunches exactly a foot before Miss Mayfield—himself a resplendent vision of flying riata, crimson scarf, fawn-colored trousers, and jingling silver spurs.

"Kin I do anythin' for ye, miss, at the Forks?"

Miss Mayfield looked up quietly. "I think not," she said indifferently, as if the flaming-Jeff was a very common occurrence.

Jeff here permitted the mare to bolt fifty yards, caught her up sharply, swung her round on her off hind heel, permitted her to paw the air once or twice with her white-stockinged fore-feet, and then, with another dash forward, pulled her up again just before she apparently took Miss Mayfield and her chair in a running leap.

"Are you sure, miss?" asked Jeff, with a flushed face and a rather lugubrious voice.

"Quite so, thank you," she said coldly, looking past this centaur to the wooded mountain beyond.

Jeff, thoroughly crushed, was pacing meekly away when a childlike voice stopped him.

"If you are going near a carpenter's shop you might get a new shutter for my window; it blew away last night."

"It did, miss?"

"Yes," said the shrill voice of Aunt Sally, from the doorway, "in course it did! Ye must be crazy, Jeff, for thar it stands in No. 8, whar ye must have put it after ye picked it up outside."

Jeff, conscious that Miss Mayfield's eyes were on his suffused face, stammered "that he would attend to it," and put spurs to the mare, eager only to escape.

It was not his only discomfiture; for the blacksmith, seeing Jeff's nervousness and anxiety, was suspicious of something wrong, as the world is apt to be, and appeased his conscience after the worldly fashion, by driving a hard bargain with the doubtful brother in affliction—the morality of a horse trade residing always with the seller. Whereby Master Jeff received only eighty dollars for horse and outfit—worth at least two hundred—and was also mulcted of forty dollars, principal and interest for past service of the blacksmith. Jeff walked home with forty dollars in his pocket—capital to prosecute his honest calling of innkeeper; the blacksmith retired to an adjoining tavern to discuss Jeff's affairs, and further reduce his credit. Yet I doubt which was the happier—the blacksmith estimating his possible gains, and doubtful of some uncertain sequence in his luck, or Jeff, temporarily relieved, boundlessly hopeful, and filled with the vague delights of a first passion. The only discontented brute in the whole transaction was poor Rabbit, who, missing certain attentions, became indignant, after the manner of her sex, bit a piece out of her crib, kicked a hole in her box, and receiving a bad character from the blacksmith, gave a worse one to her late master.

Bret Harte

Jeff's purchases were of a temporary and ornamental quality, but not always judicious as a permanent investment. Overhearing some remark from Miss Mayfield concerning the dangerous character of the two-tined steel fork, which was part of the table equipage of the "Half-way House," he purchased half a dozen of what his aunt was pleased to specify as "split spoons," and thereby lost his late good standing with her. He not only repaired the window-shutter, but tempered the glaring window itself with a bit of curtain; he half carpeted Miss Mayfield's bed-room with wild-cat skins and the now historical bear-skin, and felt himself overpaid when that young lady, passing the soft tabbyskins across her cheek, declared they were "lovely." For Miss Mayfield, deprecating slaughter in the abstract, accepted its results gratefully, like the rest of her sex, and while willing to "let the hart ungalled play," nevertheless was able to console herself with its venison. The woods, besides yielding aid and comfort of this kind to the distressed damsel, were flamboyant with vivid spring blossoms, and Jeff lit up the cold, white walls of her virgin cell with demonstrative color, and made—what his aunt, a cleanly soul, whose ideas of that quality were based upon the absence of any color whatever, called—"a litter."

The result of which was to make Miss Mayfield, otherwise lanquid and ennuye, welcome Jeff's presence with a smile; to make Jeff, otherwise anxious, eager, and keenly attentive, mute and silent in her presence. Two symptoms bad for Jeff.

Meantime Mr. Mayfield's small conventional spirit pined for fellowship, only to be found in larger civilizations, and sought, under plea of business, a visit to Sacramento, where a few of the Mayfield type, still surviving, were to be found.

This was a relief to Jeff, who only through his regard for the daughter, was kept from open quarrel with the father. He fancied Miss Mayfield felt relieved too, although Jeff had noticed that Mayfield had deferred to his daughter more often than his wife—over whom your conventional small autocrat is always victorious. It takes the legal matrimonial contract to properly develop the first-class tyrant, male or female.

On one of these days Jeff was returning through the woods from marketing at the Forks, which, since the sale of Rabbit, had became a foot-sore and tedious business. He had reached the edge of the forest, and through the wider-spaced trees, the bleak sunlit plateau of his house was beginning to open out, when he stopped instantly. I know not what Jeff had been thinking of, as he trudged along, but here, all at once, he was thrilled and possessed with the odor of some faint, foreign perfume. He flushed a little at first, and then turned pale. Now the woods were as full of as delicate, as subtle, as grateful, and, I wot, far healthier and purer odors than this; but this represented to Jeff the physical contiguity of Miss Mayfield, who had the knack—peculiar to some of her sex— of selecting a perfume that ideally identified her. Jeff looked around cautiously; at the foot of a tree hard by lay one of her wraps, still redolent of her. Jeff put down the bag which, in lieu of a market basket, he was carrying on his shoulder, and with a blushing face hid it behind a tree. It contained her dinner!

He took a few steps forwards with an assumption of ease and unconsciousness. Then he stopped, for not a hundred yards distant sat—Miss Mayfield on a mossy boulder, her cloak hanging from her shoulders, her hands clasped round her crossed knees, and one little foot out—an exasperating combination of Evangeline and little Red Riding Hood in everything, I fear, but credulousness and self-devotion. She looked up as he walked towards her (non constat that the little witch had not already seen him half a mile away!) and smiled sweetly as she looked at him. So sweetly, indeed, that poor Jeff felt like the hulking wolf of the old world fable, and hesitated—as that wolf did not. The California faunae have possibly depreciated.

"Come here!" she cried, in a small head voice, not unlike a bird's twitter.

Jeff lumbered on clumsily. His high boots had become suddenly very heavy

"I'm so glad to see you. I've just tired poor mother out—I'm always tiring people out—and she's gone back to the house to write letters. Sit down, Mr. Jeff, do, please!"

Jeff, feeling uncomfortably large in Miss Mayfield's presence, painfully seated himself on the edge of a very low stone, which had the effect of bringing his knees up on a level with his chin, and affected an ease glaringly simulated.

"Or lie down, there, Mr. Jeff—it is so comfortable."

Jeff, with a dreadful conviction that he was crashing down like a falling pine-tree, managed at last to acquire a recumbent position at a respectful distance from the little figure.

"There, isn't it nice?"

"Yes, Miss Mayfield."

"But, perhaps," said Miss Mayfield, now that she had him down, "perhaps you too have got something to do. Dear me! I'm like that naughty boy in the story-book, who went round to all the animals, in turn, asking them to play with him. He could only find the butterfly who had nothing to do. I don't wonder he was disgusted. I hate butterflies."

Love clarifies the intellect! Jeff, astonished at himself, burst out, "Why, look yer, Miss Mayfield, the butterfly only hez a day or two to—to—to live and—be happy!"

Miss Mayfield crossed her knees again, and instantly, after the sublime fashion of her sex, scattered his intellect by a swift transition from the abstract to the concrete. "But you're not a butterfly, Mr. Jeff. You're always doing something. You've been hunting."

"No-o!" said Jeff, scarlet, as he thought of his gun in pawn at the "Summit."

"But you do hunt; I know it."

"How?"

"You shot those quail for me the morning after I came. I heard you go out—early—very early."

"Why, you allowed you slept so well that night, Miss Mayfield."

"Yes; but there's a kind of delicious half-sleep that sick people have sometimes, when they know and are gratefully conscious that other people are doing things for them, and it makes them rest all the sweeter."

There was a dead silence. Jeff, thrilling all over, dared not say anything to dispel his delicious dream. Miss Mayfield, alarmed at his readiness with the butterfly illustration, stopped short. They both looked at the prospect, at the distant "Summit Hotel"—a mere snow-drift on the mountain —at the clear sunlight on the barren plateau, at the bleak, uncompromising "Half-way House," and said nothing.

"I ought to be very grateful," at last began Miss Mayfield, in quite another voice, and a suggestion that she was now approaching real and profitable conversation, "that I'm so much better. This mountain air has been like balm to me. I feel I am growing stronger day by day. I do not wonder that you are so healthy and so strong as you are, Mr. Jeff."

Jeff, who really did not know before that he was so healthy, apologetically admitted the fact. At the same time, he was miserably conscious that Miss Mayfield's condition, despite her ill health, was very superior to his own.

"A month ago," she continued reflectively, "my mother would never have thought it possible to leave me here alone. Perhaps she may be getting worried now."

Miss Mayfield had calculated over much on Jeff's recumbent position. To her surprise and slight mortification, he rose instantly to his feet, and said anxiously,

"Ef you think so, miss, p'raps I'm keeping you here."

"Not at all, Mr. Jeff. Your being here is a sufficient excuse for my staying," she replied, with the large dignity of a small body.

Jeff, mentally and physically crushed again, came down a little heavier than before, and reclined humbly at her feet. Second knock-down blow for Miss Mayfield.

"Come, Mr. Jeff," said the triumphant goddess, in her first voice, "tell me something about yourself. How do you live here—I mean; what do you do? You ride, of course—and very well too, I can tell you! But you know that. And of course that scarf and the silver spurs and the whole dashing equipage are not intended entirely for yourself. No! Some young woman is made happy by that exhibition, of course. Well, then, there's the riding down to see her, and perhaps the riding out with her, and—what else?"

"Miss Mayfield," said Jeff, suddenly rising above his elbow and his grammar, "thar isn't no young woman! Thar isn't another soul except yourself that I've laid eyes on, or cared to see since I've been yer. Ef my aunt hez been telling ye that—she's—she—she—she—she—lies."

Absolute, undiluted truth, even of a complimentary nature, is confounding to most women. Miss Mayfield was no exception to her sex. She first laughed, as she felt she ought to, and properly might with any other man than Jeff; then she got frightened, and said hurriedly, "No, no! you misunderstand me. Your aunt has said nothing." And then she stopped with a pink spot on her cheek-bones. First blood for Jeff!

Now this would never do; it was worse than the butterflies! She rose to her full height—four feet eleven and a half—and drew her cloak over her shoulders. "I think I will return to the house," she said quietly; "I suppose I ought not to over-task my strength."

"You'd better let me go with you, miss," said Jeff submissively.

"I will, on one condition," she said, recovering her archness, with a little venom in it, I fear. "You were going home, too, when I called to you. Now, I do not intend to let you leave that bag behind that tree, and then have to come back for it, just because you feel obliged to go with me. Bring it with you on one arm, and I'll take the other, or else—I'll go alone. Don't be alarmed," she added softly; "I'm stronger than I was the first night I came, when you carried me and all my worldly goods besides."

She turned upon him her subtle magnetic eyes, and looked at him as she had the first night they met. Jeff turned away bewildered, but presently appeared again with the bag on his shoulder, and her wrap on his arm. As she slipped her little hand over his sleeve, he began, apologetically and nervously,

"When I said that about Aunt Sally, miss, I"—

The hand immediately became limp, the grasp conventional.

"I was mad, miss," Jeff blundered on, "and I don't see how you believed it—knowing everything ez you do."

"How knowing everything as I do?" asked Miss Mayfield coldly.

"Why, about the quail, and about the bag!"

"Oh," said Miss Mayfield.

Five minutes later, Yuba Bill nearly ditched his coach in his utter amazement at an apparently simple spectacle—a tall, good-looking young fellow, in a red shirt and high boots, carrying a bag on his back, and beside him, hanging confidentially on his arm, a small, slight, pretty girl in a red cloak. "Nothing mean about her, eh, Bill?" said as admiring box-passenger. "Young couple, I reckon, just out from the States."

"No!" roared Bill.

"Oh, well, his sweetheart, I reckon?" suggested the box-passenger.

"Nary time!" growled Bill. "Look yer! I know 'em both, and they knows me. Did ye notiss she never drops his arm when she sees the stage comin', but kinder trapes along jist the same? Had they been courtin', she'd hev dropped his arm like pizen, and walked on t'other side the road."

Nevertheless, for some occult reason, Bill was evidently out of humor; and for the next few miles exhorted the impenitent Blue Grass horse with considerable fervor.

Meanwhile this pair, outwardly the picture of pastoral conjugality, slowly descended the hill. In that brief time, failing to get at any further facts regarding Jeff's life, or perhaps reading the story quite plainly, Miss Mayfield had twittered prettily about herself. She painted her tropic life in the Sandwich Islands—her delicious "laziness," as she called it; "for, you know," she added, "although I had the excuse of being an invalid, and of living in the laziest climate in the world, and of having money, I think, Mr. Jeff, that I'm naturally lazy. Perhaps if I lived here long enough, and got well again, I might do something, but I don't think I could ever be like your aunt. And there she is now, Mr. Jeff, making signs for you to hasten. No, don't mind me, but run on ahead; else I shall have her blaming me for demoralizing you too. Go; I insist upon it! I can walk the rest of the way alone. Will you go? You won't? Then I shall stop here and not stir another step forward until you do."

She stopped, half jestingly, half earnestly, in the middle of the road, and emphasized her determination with a nod of her head—an action that, however, shook her hat first rakishly over one eye, and then on the ground. At which Jeff laughed, picked it up, presented it to her, and then ran off to the house.

III

His aunt met him angrily on the porch. "Thar ye are at last, and yer's a stranger waitin to see you. He's been axin all sorts o' questions, about the house and the business, and kinder snoopin' round permiskiss. I don't like his looks, Jeff, but thet's no reason why ye should be gallivantin' round in business hours."

A large, thick-set man, with a mechanical smile that was an overt act of false pretense, was lounging in the bar-room. Jeff dimly remembered to have seen him at the last county election, distributing tickets at the polls. This gave Jeff a slight prejudice against him, but a greater presentiment of some vague evil in the air caused him to motion the stranger to an empty room in the angle of the house behind the barroom, which was too near the hall through which Miss Mayfield must presently pass.

It was an infelicitous act of precaution, for at that very moment Miss Mayfield slowly passed beneath its open window, and seeing her chair in the sunny angle, dropped into it for rest and possibly meditation. Consequently she overheard every word of the following colloquy.

The Stranger's voice: "Well, now, seein' ez I've been waitin' for ye over an hour, off and on, and ez my bizness with ye is two words, it strikes me yer puttin' on a little too much style in this yer interview, Mr. Jefferson Briggs."

Jeff's voice (a little husky with restraint): "What is yer business?"

The stranger's voice (lazily): "It's an attachment on this yer property for principal, interest, and costs—one hundred and twelve dollars and' seventy-five cents, at the suit of Cyrus Parker."

Jeff's voice (in quick surprise): "Parker? Why, I saw him only yesterday, and he agreed to wait a spell longer."

The Stranger's voice: "Mebbee he did! Mebbee he heard afterwards suthin' about the goin's on up yar. Mebbee he heard suthin' o' property bein' converted into ready cash— sich property ez horses, guns, and sich! Mebbee he heard o' gay and festive doin's—chickin every day, fresh eggs, butcher's meat, port wine, and sich! Mebbee he allowed that his chances o' gettin' his own honest grub outer his debt was lookin' mighty slim! Mebbee" (louder) "he thought he'd ask the man who bought yer horse, and the man you pawned your gun to, what was goin' on! Mebbee he thought he'd like to get a holt a suthin' himself, even if it was only some of that yar chickin and port wine!"

Jeff's voice (earnestly and hastily): "They're not for me. I have a family boarding here, with a sick daughter. You don't think—"

The Stranger's voice (lazily): "I reckon! I seed you and her pre-ambulating down the hill, lockin' arms. A good deal o' style, Jeff—fancy! expensive! How does Aunt Sally take it?"

A slight shaking of the floor and window—a dead silence.

Bret Harte

The Stranger's voice (very faintly): "For God's sake, let me up!"

Jeff's voice (very distinctly): "Another word! raise your voice above a whisper, and by the living G—"

Silence.

The Stranger's voice (gasping): "I—I—promise!"

Jeff's voice (low and desperate): "Get up out of that! Sit down thar! Now hear me! I'm not resisting your process. If you had all h-ll as witnesses you daren't say that. I've shut up your foul jaw, and kept it from poisoning the air, and thar's no law in Californy agin it! Now listen. What! You will, will you?"

Everything quiet; a bird twittering on the window ledge, nothing more.

The Stranger's voice (very huskily): "I cave! Gimme some whiskey."

Jeff's voice: "When we're through. Now listen! You can take possession of the house; you can stand behind the bar and take every cent that comes in; you can prevent anything going out; but as long as Mr. Mayfield and his family stay here, by the living God—law or no law—I'll be boss here, and they shall never know it!"

The Stranger's voice (weakly and submissively): "That sounds square. Anythin' not agin the law and in reason, Jeff!"

Jeff's voice: "I mean to be square. Here is all the money I have, ten dollars. Take it for any extra trouble you may have to satisfy me."

A pause—the clinking of coin.

The Stranger's voice (deprecatingly): "Well! I reckon that would be about fair. Consider the trouble" (a weak laugh here) "just now. 'Tain't every man ez hez your grip. He! he! Ef ye hadn't took me so suddent like—he! he!—well!—how about that ar whiskey?"

Jeff's voice (coolly): "I'll bring it."

Steps, silence, coughing, spitting, and throat-clearing from the stranger.

Steps again, and the click of glass.

The Stranger's voice (submissively): "In course I must go back to the Forks and fetch up my duds. Ye know what I mean! Thar now—don't, Mr. Jeff!"

Jeff's voice (sternly): "If I find you go back on me—"

The Stranger's voice (hurriedly): "Thar's my hand on it. Ye can count on Jim Dodd."

Steps again. Silence. A bird lights on the window ledge, and peers into the room. All is at rest.

Jeff and the deputy-sheriff walked through the bar-room and out on the porch. Miss Mayfield in an arm-chair looked up from her book.

"I've written a letter to my father that I'd like to have mailed at the Forks this afternoon," she said, looking from Jeff to the stranger; "perhaps this gentleman will oblige me by taking it, if he's going that way."

"I'll take it, miss," said Jeff hurriedly.

"No," said Miss Mayfield archly, "I've taken up too much of your time already."

"I'm at your service, miss," said the stranger, considerably affected by the spectacle of this pretty girl, who certainly at that moment, in her bright eyes and slightly pink cheeks, belied the suggestion of ill health.

"Thank you. Dear me!" She was rummaging in a reticule and in her pocket, etc. "Oh, Mr. Jeff!"

"Yes, miss?"

"I'm so frightened!"

"How, miss?"

"I have—yes!—I have left that letter on the stump in the woods, where I was sitting when you came. Would you—"

Jeff darted into the house, seized his hat, and stopped. He was thinking of the stranger.

"Could you be so kind?"

Jeff looked in her agitated face, cast a meaning glance at the stranger, and was off like a shot.

The fire dropped out of Miss Mayfield's eyes and cheeks. She turned toward the stranger.

"Please step this way."

She always hated her own childish treble. But just at that

moment she thought she had put force and dignity into it, and was correspondingly satisfied. The deputy sheriff was equally pleased, and came towards the upright little figure with open admiration.

"Your name is Dodd—James Dodd?"

"Yes, miss."

"You are the deputy sheriff of the county? Don't look round—there is no one here!"

"Well, miss—if you say so—yes!"

"My father—Mr. Mayfield—understood so. I regret he is not here. I regret still more I could not have seen you before you saw Mr. Briggs, as he wished me to."

"Yes, miss."

"My father is a friend of Mr. Briggs, and knows something of his affairs. There was a debt to a Mr. Parker" (here Miss Mayfield apparently consulted an entry in her tablets) "of one hundred and twelve dollars and seventy-five cents—am I right?"

The deputy, with great respect: "That is the figgers."

"Which he wished to pay without the knowledge of Mr. Briggs, who would not have consented to it."

The official opened his eyes. "Yes, miss."

"Well, as Mr. Mayfield is NOT here, I am here to pay it for him. You can take a check on Wells, Fargo & Co., I suppose?"

"Certainly, miss."

She took a check-book and pen and ink from her reticule, and filled up a check. She handed it to him, and the pen and ink. "You are to give me a receipt."

The deputy looked at the matter-of-fact little figure, and signed and handed over the receipted bill.

"My father said Mr. Briggs was not to know this."

"Certainly not, miss."

"It was Mr. Briggs's intention to let the judgment take its course, and give up the house. You are a man of business, Mr. Dodd, and know that this is ridiculous!"

The deputy laughed. "In course, miss."

"And whatever Mr. Briggs may have proposed to you to do, when you go back to the Forks, you are to write him a letter, and say that you will simply hold the judgment without levy."

"All right, miss," said the deputy, not ill-pleased to hold himself in this superior attitude to Jeff.

"And—"

"Yes, miss?"

She looked steadily at him. "Mr. Briggs told my father that he would pay you ten dollars for the privilege of staying here."

"Yes, miss."

"And, of course, THAT'S not necessary now."

"No-o, miss."

A very small white hand—a mere child's hand—was here extended, palm uppermost.

The official, demoralized completely, looked at it a moment, then went into his pockets and counted out into the palm the coins given by Jeff; they completely filled the tiny receptacle.

Miss Mayfield counted the money gravely, and placed it in her portemonnaie with a snap.

Certain qualities affect certain natures. This practical business act of the diminutive beauty before him—albeit he was just ten dollars out of pocket by it—struck the official into helpless admiration. He hesitated.

"That's all," said Miss Mayfield coolly; "you need not wait. The letter was only an excuse to get Mr. Briggs out of the way."

"I understand ye, miss." He hesitated still. "Do you reckon to stop in these parts long?"

"I don't know."

"'Cause ye ought to come down some day to the Forks."

"Yes."

"Good morning, miss."

"Good morning."

Yet at the corner of the house the rascal turned and looked back at the little figure in the sunlight. He had just been physically overcome by a younger man—he had lost ten dollars—he had a wife and three children. He forgot all this. He had been captivated by Miss Mayfield!

That practical heroine sat there five minutes. At the end of that time Jeff came bounding down the hill, his curls damp with perspiration; his fresh, honest face the picture of woe, HER woe, for the letter could not be found!

"Never mind, Mr. Jeff. I wrote another and gave it to him."

Two tears were standing on her cheeks. Jeff turned white.

"Good God, miss!"

"It's nothing. You were right, Mr. Jeff! I ought not to have walked down here alone. I'm very, very tired, and—so—so miserable."

What woman could withstand the anguish of that honest boyish face? I fear Miss Mayfield could, for she looked at him over her handkerchief, and said: "Perhaps you had something to say to your friend, and I've sent him off."

"Nothing," said Jeff hurriedly; and she saw that all his other troubles had vanished at the sight of her weakness. She rose tremblingly from her seat. "I think I will go in now, but I think—I think—I must ask you to—to—carry me!"

Oh, lame and impotent conclusion!

The next moment, Jeff, pale, strong, passionate, but tender as a mother, lifted her in his arms and brought her into the sitting-room. A simultaneous ejaculation broke from Aunt

Sally and Mrs. Mayfield—the possible comment of posterity on the whole episode.

"Well, Jeff, I reckoned you'd be up to suthin' like that!"

"Well, Jessie! I knew you couldn't be trusted."

Mr. James Dodd did not return from the Forks that afternoon, to Jeff's vague uneasiness. Towards evening a messenger brought a note from him, written on the back of a printed legal form, to this effect:

DEAR SIR—Seeing as you Intend to act on the Square in regard to that little Mater I have aranged Things so that I ant got to stop with you but I'll drop in onct in a wile to keep up a show for a Drink—respy yours, J. DODD.

In this latter suggestion our legal Cerberus exhibited all three of his heads at once. One could keep faith with Miss Mayfield, one could see her "onct in a wile," and one could drink at Jeff's expense. Innocent Jeff saw only generosity and kindness in the man he had half-choked, and a sense of remorse and shame almost outweighed the relief of his absence. "He might hev been ugly," said Jeff. He did not know how, in this selfish world, there is very little room for gratuitous, active ugliness.

Miss Mayfield did not leave her room that afternoon. The wind was getting up, and it was growing dark when Jeff, idly sitting on his porch, hoping for her appearance, was quite astounded at the apparition of Yuba Bill as a pedestrian, dusty and thirsty, making for his usual refreshment. Jeff brought out the bottle, but could not refrain from mixing his verbal astonishment with the conventional cocktail. Bill, partaking of his liquor and becoming once more a speaking animal, slowly drew off his heavy, baggy driving gloves. No one had ever seen Bill without them—he was currently believed to sleep in them—and when he laid them on the counter they still retained the grip of his hand, which gave them an entertaining likeness to two plethoric and overfed spiders.

"Ef I concluded to pass over my lines to a friend and take a pasear up yer this evening," said Bill, eying Jeff sharply, "I don't know ez thar's any law agin it! Onless yer keepin' a private branch o' the Occidental Ho-tel, and on'y take in fash'n'ble fammerlies!"

Jeff, with a rising color, protested against such a supposition.

"Because ef ye ARE," said Bill, lifting his voice, and crushing one of the overgrown spiders with his fist, "I've got a word or two to say to the son of Joe Briggs of Tuolumne. Yes, sir! Joe Briggs—yer father—ez blew his brains out for want of a man ez could stand up and say a word to him at the right time."

"Bill," said Jeff, in a low, resolute tone—that tone yielded up only from the smitten chords of despair and desperation— "thar's a sick woman in the house. I'll listen to anything you've got to say if you'll say it quietly. But you must and SHALL speak low."

Real men quickly recognize real men the world over; it is only your shams who fence and spar. Bill, taking in the voice of the speaker more than his words, dropped his own.

"I said I had a kepple of words to say to ye. Thar isn't any time in the last fower months—ever since ye took stock in this old shanty, for the matter o' that—that I couldn't hev said them to ye. I've knowed all your doin's. I've knowed all your debts, 'spesh'ly that ye owe that sneakin' hound Parker; and thar isn't a time that I couldn't and wouldn't hev chipped in and paid 'em for ye—for your father's sake—ef I'd allowed it to be the square thing for ye. But I know ye, Jeff. I know what's in your BLOOD. I knew your father—allus dreamin', hopin,' waitin'; I know YOU, Jeff, dreamin', hopin', waitin' till the end. And I stood by, givin' you a free rein, and let it come!"

Jeff buried his face in his hands.

"It ain't your blame—it's blood! It ain't a week ago ez the kimpany passes me over a hoss. 'Three-quarters Morgan,' sez they. Sez I: 'Wot's the other quarter?' Sez they: 'A Mexican half-breed.' Well, she was a fair sort of hoss. Comin' down Heavytree Hill last trip, we meets a drove o' Spanish steers. In course she goes wild directly. Blood!"

Bill raised his glass, softly swirled its contents round and round, tasted it, and set it down.

"The kepple o' words I had to say to ye was this: Git up and git!"

Something like this had passed through Jeff's mind the day before the Mayfields came. Something like it had haunted him once or twice since. He turned quickly upon the speaker.

"Ez how? you sez," said Bill, catching at the hook. "I drives up yer some night, and you sez to me, 'Bill, hev you got two seats over to the Divide for me and aunty—out on a pasear.' And I sez, 'I happen to hev one inside and one on the box with me.' And you hands out yer traps and any vallybles ye don't want ter leave, and you puts your aunt inside, and gets up on the box with me. And you sez to me, ez man to man, 'Bill,' sez you, 'might you hev a kepple o' hundred dollars about ye that ye could lend a man ez was leaving the county, dead broke?' and I sez, 'I've got it, and I know of an op'nin' for such a man in the next county.' And you steps into THAT op'nin', and your creditors—'spesh'ly Parker—slips into THIS, and in a week they offers to settle with ye ten cents on the dollar."

Jeff started, flushed, trembled, recovered himself, and after a moment said, doggedly: "I can't do it, Bill; I couldn't."

"In course," said Bill, putting his hands slowly into his pockets, and stretching his legs out—"in course ye can't because of a woman!"

Jeff turned upon him like a hunted bear. Both men rose, but Bill already had his hand on Jeff's shoulder.

"I reckoned a minute ago there was a sick gal in the house! Who's going to make a row now! Who's going to stamp and tear round, eh?"

Jeff sank back on his chair.

"I said thar was a woman," continued Bill; "thar allus is one! Let a man be hell-bent or heaven-bent, somewhere in his track is a woman's feet. I don't say anythin' agin this gal, ez a gal. The best of 'em, Jeff, is only guide-posts to p'int a fellow on his right road, and only a fool or a drunken man holds on to 'em or leans agin em. Allowin' this gal is all you think she is, how far is your guide-post goin' with ye, eh? Is she goin' to leave her father and mother for ye? Is she goin' to give up herself and her easy ways and her sicknesses for ye? Is she willin' to take ye for a perpetooal landlord the rest of her life? And if she is, Jeff, are ye the man to let her? Are ye willin' to run on her errants, to fetch her dinners ez ye do? Thar ez men ez does it; not yer in Californy, but over in the States thar's fellows is willing to take that situation. I've heard," continued Bill, in a low, mysterious voice, as of one describing the habits of the Anthropophagi—"I've heard o' fellows ez call themselves men, sellin' of themselves to rich women in that way. I've heard o' rich gals buyin' of men for their shape; sometimes—but thet's in furrin' kintries—for their pedigree! I've heard o' fellows bein' in that business, and callin' themselves men instead o' hosses! Ye ain't that kind o' man, Jeff. 'Tain't in yer blood. Yer father was a fool about women, and in course they ruined him, as they allus do the best men. It's on'y the fools and sneaks ez a woman ever makes anythin' out of. When ye hear of a man a woman hez made, ye hears of a nincompoop. And when they does produce 'em in the way o' nater, they ain't responsible for 'em, and sez they're the image o' their fathers! Ye ain't a man ez is goin' to trust yer fate to a woman!"

"No," said Jeff darkly.

"I reckoned not," said Bill, putting his hands in his pockets again. "Ye might if ye was one o' them kind o' fellows as kem up from 'Frisco with her to Sacramento. One o' them kind o' fellows ez could sling poetry and French and Latin to her—one of HER kind—but ye ain't! No, sir!"

Unwise William of Yuba! In any other breast but Jeff's that random shot would have awakened the irregular auxiliary of love—jealousy! But Jeff, being at once proud and humble, had neither vanity nor conceit, without which jealousy is impossible. Yet he winced a little, for he had feeling, and then said earnestly:

"Do you think that opening you spoke of would hold for a day or two longer?"

"I reckon."

"Well, then, I think I can settle up matters here my own way, and go with you, Bill."

He had risen, and yet hesitatingly kept his hand on the back of his chair. "Bill!"

"Jeff!"

"I want to ask you a question; speak up, and don't mind me, but say the truth."

Our crafty Ulysses, believing that he was about to be entrapped, ensconced himself in his pockets, cocked one eye, and said: "Go on, Jeff."

"Was my father VERY bad?"

Bill took his hands from his pockets. "Thar isn't a man ez crawls above his grave ez is worthy to lie in the same ground with him!"

"Thank you, Bill. Good night; I'm going to turn in!"

"Look yar, boy! G-d d—n it all, Jeff! what do ye mean?"

There were two tears—twin sisters of those in his sweetheart's eyes that afternoon—now standing in Jeff's!

Bill caught both his hands in his own. Had they been of the Latin race they would have, right honestly, taken each other in their arms, and perhaps kissed! Being Anglo-Saxons, they gripped each other's hands hard, and one, as above stated, swore!

When Jeff ascended to his room that night he went directly to his trunk and took out Miss Mayfield's slipper. Alack!

during the day Aunt Sally had "put things to rights" in his room, and the trunk had been moved. This had somewhat disordered its contents, and Miss Mayfield's slipper contained a dozen shot from a broken Eley's cartridge, a few quinine pills, four postage stamps, part of a coral earring which Jeff—on the most apocryphal authority—fondly believed belonged to his mother, whom he had never seen, and a small silver school medal which Jeff had once received for "good conduct," much to his own surprise, but which he still religiously kept as evidence of former conventional character. He colored a little, rubbed the medal and earring ruefully on his sleeve, replaced them in his trunk, and then hastily emptied the rest of the slipper's contents on the floor. This done, he drew off his boots, and, gliding noiselessly down the stair, hung the slipper on the knob of Miss Mayfield's door, and glided back again without detection.

Rolling himself in his blankets, he lay down on his bed. But not to sleep! Staringly wide awake, he at last felt the lulling of the wind that nightly shook his casement, and listened while the great, rambling, creaking, disjointed "Half-way House" slowly settled itself to repose. He thought of many things; of himself, of his past, of his future, but chiefly, I fear, of the pale proud face now sleeping contentedly in the chamber below him. He tossed with many plans and projects, more or less impracticable, and then began to doze. Whereat the moon, creeping in the window, laid a cold white arm across him, and eventually dried a few foolish tears upon his sleeping lashes.

IV

Aunt Sally was making pies in the kitchen the next morning when Jeff hesitatingly stole upon her. The moment was not a felicitous one. Pie-making was usually an aggressive pursuit with Aunt Sally, entered into severely, and prosecuted unto the bitter end. After watching her a few moments Jeff came up and placed his arms tenderly around her. People very much in love find relief, I am told, in this vicarious expression.

"Aunty."

"Well, Jeff! Thar, now—yer gittin' all dough!" Nevertheless, the hard face relaxed a little. Something of a smile stole round her mouth, showing what she might have been before theology and bitters had supplied the natural feminine longings.

"Aunty dear!"

"You—boy!"

It WAS a boy's face—albeit bearded like the pard, with an extra fierceness in the mustaches—that looked upon hers. She could not help bestowing a grim floury kiss upon it.

"Well, what is it now?"

"I'm thinking, aunty, it's high time you and me packed up our traps and 'shook' this yar shanty, and located somewhere else." Jeff's voice was ostentatiously cheerful, but his eyes were a little anxious.

"What for NOW?"

Jeff hastily recounted his ill luck, and the various reasons—excepting of course the dominant one—for his resolution.

"And when do you kalkilate to go?"

"If you'll look arter things here," hesitated Jeff, "I reckon I'll go up along with Bill to-morrow, and look round a bit."

"And how long do you reckon that gal would stay here after yar gone?"

This was a new and startling idea to Jeff. But in his humility he saw nothing in it to flatter his conceit. Rather the reverse. He colored, and then said apologetically,—

"I thought that you and Jinny could get along without me. The butcher will pack the provisions over from the Fork."

Laying down her rolling-pin, Aunt Sally turned upon Jeff with ostentatious deliberation. "Ye ain't," she began slowly, "ez taking a man with wimmen ez your father was—that's a fact, Jeff Briggs! They used to say that no woman as he went for could get away from him. But ye don't mean to say yer think yer not good enough—such as ye are—for this snip of an old maid, ez big as a gold dollar, and as yaller?"

"Aunty," said Jeff, dropping his boyish manner, and his color as suddenly, "I'd rather ye wouldn't talk that way of Miss Mayfield. Ye don't know her; and there's times," he added, with a sigh, "ez I reckon ye don't quite know ME either. That young lady, bein' sick, likes to be looked after. Any one can do that for her. She don't mind who it is. She don't care for me except for that, and," added Jeff humbly, "it's quite natural."

"I didn't say she did," returned Aunt Sally viciously; "but seeing ez you've got an empty house yer on yer hands, and me a-slavin' here on jist nothin', if this gal, for the sake o' gallivantin' with ye for a spell, chooses to stay here and keep her family here, and pay high for it, I don't see why it ain't yer duty to Providence and me to take advantage of it."

Jeff raised his eyes to his aunt's face. For the first time it struck him that she might be his father's sister and yet have no blood in her veins that answered to his. There are few shocks more startling and overpowering to original natures than this sudden sense of loneliness. Jeff could not speak, but remained looking fiercely at her.

Aunt Sally misinterpreted his silence, and returned to her work on the pies. "The gal ain't no fool," she continued, rolling out the crust as if she were laying down broad propositions. "SHE reckons on it too, ez if it was charged in the bill with the board and lodging. Why, didn't she say to me, last night, that she kalkilated afore she went away to bring up some friends from 'Frisco for a few days' visit? and didn't she say, in that pipin', affected voice o' hers, 'I oughter make some return for yer kindness and yer nephew's kindness, Aunt Sally, by showing people that can help you, and keep your house full, how pleasant it is up here.' She ain't no fool, with all her faintin's and dyin's away! No, Jeff Briggs. And if she wants to show ye off agin them city fellows ez she knows, and ye ain't got spunk enough to stand up and show off with her—why"—she turned her head impatiently, but he was gone.

If Jeff had ever wavered in his resolution he would have been steady enough NOW. But he had never wavered; the convictions and resolutions of suddenly awakened character are seldom moved by expediency. He was eager to taste the bitter dregs of his cup at once. He began to pack his trunk, and make his preparations for departure. Without avoiding Miss Mayfield in this new excitement, he no longer felt the need of her presence. He had satisfied his feverish anxieties by placing his trunk in the hall beside his open door, and was sitting on his bed, wrestling with a faded and overtasked carpet-bag that would not close and accept his hard conditions, when a small voice from the staircase thrilled him. He walked to the corridor, and, looking down, beheld Miss Mayfield midway on the steps of the staircase.

She had never looked so beautiful before! Jeff had only seen her in those soft enwrappings and half-deshabille that belong to invalid femininity. Always refined and modest thus, in her present walking-costume there was added a slight touch of coquettish adornment. There was a brightness of color in her cheek and eye, partly the result of climbing the staircase, partly the result of that audacious impulse that had led her— a modest virgin—to seek a gentleman in this personal fashion. Modesty in a young girl has a comfortable satisfying charm, recognized easily by all humanity; but he must be a sorry knave or a worse prig who is not deliciously thrilled when Modesty puts her charming little foot just over the threshold of Propriety.

"The mountain would not come to Mohammed, so Mohammed must come to the mountain," said Miss Mayfield. "Mother is asleep, Aunt Sally is at work in the kitchen, and here am I, already dressed for a ramble in this bright afternoon sunshine, and no one to go with me. But, perhaps, you, too, are busy?"

"No, miss. I will be with you in a moment."

I wish I could say that he went back to calm his pulses, which the dangerous music of Miss Mayfield's voice had set to throbbing, by a few moments' calm and dispassionate reflection. But he only returned to brush his curls out of his eyes and ears, and to button over his blue flannel shirt a white linen collar, which he thought might better harmonize with Miss Mayfield's attire.

She was sitting on the staircase, poking her parasol through the balusters. "You need not have taken that trouble, Mr. Jeff," she said pleasantly. "YOU are a part of this mountain picture at all times; but I am obliged to think of dress."

"It was no trouble, miss."

Something in the tone of his voice made her look in his face as she rose. It was a trifle paler, and a little older. The result, doubtless, thought Miss Mayfield, of his yesterday's experience with the deputy-sheriff.

Such was her rapid deduction. Nevertheless, after the fashion of her sex, she immediately began to argue from quite another hypothesis.

"You are angry with me, Mr. Jeff."

"What, I—Miss Mayfield?"

"Yes, you!"

"Miss Mayfield!"

"Oh yes, you are. Don't deny it?"

"Upon my soul—"

"Yes! You give me punishments and—penances!"

Jeff opened his blue eyes on his tormentor. Could Aunt Sally have been saying anything?

"If anybody, Miss Mayfield—" he began.

"Nobody but you. Look here!"

She extended her little hand with a smile. In the centre of her palm lay four shining double B SHOT.

"There! I found those in my slipper this morning!" Jeff was speechless.

"Of course YOU did it! Of course it was YOU who found my slipper!" said Miss Mayfield, laughing. "But why did you put shot in it, Mr. Jeff? In some Catholic countries, when people have done wrong, the priests make them do penance by walking with peas in their shoes! What have I ever done to you? And why SHOT? They're ever so much harder than peas."

Seeing only the mischievous, laughing face before him, and the open palm containing the damning evidence of the broken Eley's cartridge, Jeff stammered out the truth.

"I found the slipper in the bear-skin, Miss Mayfield. I put it in my trunk to keep, thinking yer wouldn't miss it, and it's being a kind of remembrance after you're gone away—of— of the night you came here. Somebody moved the trunk in my room," and he hung his head here. "The things inside all got mixed up."

"And that made you change your mind about keeping it?" said Miss Mayfield, still smiling.

"No, miss."

"What was it, then?"

"I gave it back to you, Miss Mayfield, because I was going away."

"Indeed! Where?"

"I'm going to find another location. Maybe you've noticed," he continued, falling back into his old apologetic manner in spite of his pride of resolution—"maybe you've noticed that this place here has no advantages for a hotel."

"I had not, indeed. I have been very comfortable."

"Thank you, miss."

"When do you go?"

"To-night."

For all his pride and fixed purpose he could not help looking eagerly in her face. Miss Mayfield's eyes met his pleasantly and quietly.

"I'm sorry to part with you so soon," she said, as she stepped back a pace or two with folded hands. "Of course every moment of your time now is occupied. You must not think of wasting it on me."

But Jeff had recovered his sad composure. "I'd like to go with you, Miss Mayfield. It's the last time, you know," he added simply.

Miss Mayfield did not reply. It was a tacit assent, however, although she moved somewhat stiffly at his side as they walked towards the door. Quite convinced that Jeff's resolution came from his pecuniary troubles, Miss Mayfield was wondering if she had not better assure him of his security from further annoyance from Dodd. Wonderful complexity of female intellect! she was a little hurt at his ingratitude to her for a kindness he could not possibly have known. Miss Mayfield felt that in some way she was unjustly treated. How many of our miserable sex, incapable of divination, have been crushed under that unreasonable feminine reproof, "You ought to have known!"

The afternoon sun was indeed shining brightly as they stepped out before the bleak angle of the "Half-way House"; but it failed to mitigate the habitually practical austerity of the mountain breeze—a fact which Miss Mayfield had never before noticed. The house was certainly bleak and exposed; the site by no means a poetical one. She wondered if she had not put a romance into it, and perhaps even into the man beside her, which did not belong to either. It was a moment of dangerous doubt.

"I don't know but that you're right, Mr. Jeff," she said finally, as they faced the hill, and began the ascent together. "This place is a little queer, and bleak, and—unattractive."

"Yes, miss," said Jeff, with direct simplicity, "I've always wondered what you saw in it to make you content to stay, when it would be so much prettier, and more suitable for you at the 'Summit.'"

Miss Mayfield bit her lip, and was silent. After a few moments' climbing she said, almost pettishly, "Where is this famous 'Summit'?"

Jeff stopped. They had reached the top of the hill. He pointed across an olive-green chasm to a higher level, where, basking in the declining sun, clustered the long rambling outbuildings around the white blinking facade of the "Summit House." Framed in pines and hemlocks, tender with soft gray shadows, and nestling beyond a foreground of cultivated slope, it was a charming rustic picture.

Miss Mayfield's quick eye took in its details. Her quick intellect took in something else. She had seated herself on the road-bank, and, clasping her knees between her locked fingers, she suddenly looked up at Jeff. "What possessed you to come half-way up a mountain, instead of going on to the top?"

"Poverty, miss!"

Miss Mayfield flushed a little at this practical direct answer to her half-figurative question. However, she began to think that moral Alpine-climbing youth might have pecuniary restrictions in their high ambitions, and that the hero of "Excelsior" might have succumbed to more powerful opposition than the wisdom of Age or the blandishments of Beauty.

"You mean that poverty up there is more expensive?"

"Yes, miss."

"But you would like to live there?"

"Yes."

They were both silent. Miss Mayfield glanced at Jeff under the corners of her lashes. He was leaning against a tree, absorbed in thought. Accustomed to look upon him as a pleasing picturesque object, quite fresh, original, and characteristic, she was somewhat disturbed to find that to-day he presented certain other qualities which clearly did not agree with her preconceived ideas of his condition. He had abandoned his usual large top-boots for low shoes, and she could not help noticing that his feet were small and slender as were his hands, albeit browned by exposure. His ruddy color was gone too, and his face, pale with sorrow and experience, had a new expression. His buttoned-up coat and white collar, so unlike his usual self, also had its suggestions—which Miss Mayfield was at first inclined to resent. Women are quick to notice and augur more or less wisely from these small details. Nevertheless, she began in quite another tone.

"Do you remember your mother—MR.—MR.—BRIGGS?"

Jeff noticed the new epithet. "No, miss; she died when I was quite young."

"Your father, then?"

Jeff's eye kindled a little, aggressively. "I remember HIM."

"What was he?"

"Miss Mayfield!"

"What was his business or profession?"

"He—hadn't—any!"

"Oh, I see—a gentleman of property."

Jeff hesitated, looked at Miss Mayfield hurriedly, colored, and did not reply.

"And lost his property, Mr. Briggs?" With one of those rare impulses of an overtasked gentle nature, Jeff turned upon her almost savagely. "My father was a gambler, and shot himself at a gambling table."

Miss Mayfield rose hurriedly. "I—I beg your pardon, Mr. Jeff."

Jeff was silent.

"You know—you MUST know—I did not mean—"

No reply.

"Mr. Jeff!"

Her little hand fluttered toward him, and lit upon his sleeve, where it was suddenly captured and pressed passionately to his lips.

"I did not mean to be thoughtless or unkind," said Miss Mayfield, discreetly keeping to the point, and trying weakly to disengage her hand. "You know I wouldn't hurt your feelings."

"I know, Miss Mayfield." (Another kiss.)

"I was ignorant of your history."

"Yes, miss." (A kiss.)

"And if I could do anything for you, Mr. Jeff—" She stopped.

It was a very trying position. Being small, she was drawn after her hand quite up to Jeff's shoulder, while he, assenting in monosyllables, was parting the fingers, and kissing them separately. Reasonable discourse in this attitude was out of the question. She had recourse to strategy.

"Oh!"

"Miss Mayfield!"

"You hurt my hand."

Jeff dropped it instantly. Miss Mayfield put it in the pocket of her sacque for security. Besides, it had been so bekissed that it seemed unpleasantly conscious.

"I wish you would tell me all about yourself," she went on, with a certain charming feminine submission of manner quite unlike her ordinary speech; "I should like to help you. Perhaps I can. You know I am quite independent; I mean—"

She paused, for Jeff's face betrayed no signs of sympathetic following.

"I mean I am what people call rich in my own right. I can do as I please with my own. If any of your trouble, Mr. Jeff, arises from want of money, or capital; if any consideration of that kind takes you away from your home; if I could save you THAT TROUBLE, and find for you—perhaps a little nearer—that which you are seeking, I would be so glad to do it. You will find the world very wide, and very cold, Mr. Jeff," she continued, with a certain air of practical superiority quite natural to her, but explicable to her friends and acquaintances only as the consciousness of pecuniary independence; "and I wish you would be frank with me. Although I am a woman, I know something of business."

"I will be frank with you, miss," said Jeff, turning a colorless face upon her. "If you was ez rich as the Bank of California, and could throw your money on any fancy or whim that struck you at the moment; if you felt you could buy up any man and woman in California that was willing to be bought up; and if me and my aunt were starving in the road, we wouldn't touch the money that we hadn't earned fairly, and didn't belong to us. No, miss, I ain't that sort o' man!"

How much of this speech, in its brusqueness and slang, was an echo of Yuba Bill's teaching, how much of it was a part of Jeff's inward weakness, I cannot say. He saw Miss Mayfield recoil from him. It added to his bitterness that his thought, for the first time voiced, appeared to him by no means as effective or powerful as he had imagined it would be, but he could not recede from it; and there was the relief that the worst had come, and was over now.

Miss Mayfield took her hand out of her pocket. "I don't think you quite understand me, Mr. Jeff," she said quietly; "and I HOPE I don't understand you." She walked stiffly at his side for a few moments, but finally took the other side of the road. They had both turned, half unconsciously, back again to the "Half-way House."

Jeff felt, like all quarrel-seekers, righteous or unrighteous, the full burden of the fight. If he could have relieved his mind, and at the next moment leaped upon Yuba Bill's coach, and so passed away—without a further word of explanation—all would have been well. But to walk back with this girl, whom he had just shaken off, and who must now thoroughly hate him, was something he had not preconceived, in that delightful forecast of the imagination, when we determine what WE shall say and do without the least consideration of what may be said or done to us in return. No quarrel proceeds exactly as we expect; people have such a way of behaving illogically! And here was Miss Mayfield, who was clearly derelict, and who should have acted under that conviction, walking along on the other side of the road, trailing the splendor of her parasol in the dust like an offended goddess.

They had almost reached the house. "At what time do you go, Mr. Briggs?" asked the young lady quietly.

"At eleven to-night, by the up stage."

"I expect some friends by that stage—coming with my father."

"My aunt will take good care of them," said Jeff, a little bitterly.

"I have no doubt," responded Miss Mayfield gravely; "but I was not thinking of that. I had hoped to introduce them to you to-morrow. But I shall not be up so late to-night. And I had better say good-by to you now."

She extended the unkissed hand. Jeff took it, but presently let the limp fingers fall through his own.

"I wish you good fortune, Mr. Briggs."

She made a grave little bow, and vanished into the house. But here, I regret to say, her lady-like calm also vanished. She upbraided her mother peevishly for obliging her to seek the escort of Mr. Briggs in her necessary exercise, and flung herself with an injured air upon the sofa.

"But I thought you liked this Mr. Briggs. He seems an accommodating sort of person."

"Very accommodating. Going away just as we are expecting company!"

"Going away?" said Mrs. Mayfield in alarm. "Surely he must be told that we expect some preparation for our friends?"

"Oh," said Miss Mayfield quickly, "his aunt will arrange THAT."

Mrs. Mayfield, habitually mystified at her daughter's moods, said no more. She, however, fulfilled her duty conscientiously by rising, throwing a wrap over the young girl, tucking it in at her feet, and having, as it were, drawn a charitable veil over her peculiarities, left her alone.

At half past ten the coach dashed up to the "Half-way House," with a flash of lights and a burst of cheery voices. Jeff, coming upon the porch, was met by Mr. Mayfield, accompanying a lady and two gentlemen,—evidently the guests alluded to by his daughter. Accustomed as Jeff had become to Mr. Mayfield's patronizing superiority, it seemed unbearable now, and the easy indifference of the guests to his own presence touched him with a new bitterness. Here were HER friends, who were to take his place. It was a relief to grasp Yuba Bill's large hand and stand with him alone beside the bar.

"I'm ready to go with you to-night, Bill," said Jeff, after a pause.

Bill put down his glass—a sign of absorbing interest.

"And these yar strangers I fetched?"

"Aunty will take care of them. I've fixed everything."

Bill laid both his powerful hands on Jeff's shoulders, backed him against the wall, and surveyed him with great gravity.

"Briggs's son clar through! A little off color, but the grit all thar! Bully for you, Jeff." He wrung Jeff's hand between his own.

"Bill!" said Jeff hesitatingly.

"Jeff!"

"You wouldn't mind my getting up on the box NOW, before all the folks get round?"

"I reckon not. Thar's the box-seat all ready for ye."

Climbing to his high perch, Jeff, indistinguishable in the darkness, looked out upon the porch and the moving figures of the passengers, on Bill growling out his orders to his active hostler, and on the twinkling lights of the hotel windows. In the mystery of the night and the bitterness of his heart, everything looked strange. There was a light in Miss Mayfield's room, but the curtains were drawn. Once he thought they moved, but then, fearful of the fascination of watching them, he turned his face resolutely away.

Then, to his relief, the hour came; the passengers re-entered the coach; Bill had mounted the box, and was slowly gathering his reins, when a shrill voice rose from the porch.

"Oh, Jeff!"

Jeff leaned an anxious face out over the coach lamps.

It was Aunt Sally, breathless and on tiptoe, reaching with a letter. "Suthin' you forgot!" Then, in a hoarse stage whisper, perfectly audible to every one: "From HER!"

Jeff seized the letter with a burning face. The whip snapped, and the stage plunged forward into the darkness. Presently Yuba Bill reached down, coolly detached one of the coach lamps, and handed it to Jeff without a word.

Jeff tore open the envelope. It contained Cyrus Parker's bill receipted, and the writ Another small inclosure contained ten dollars, and a few lines written in pencil in a large masculine business hand. By the light of the lamp Jeff read as follows:—

"I hope you will forgive me for having tried to help you even in this accidental way, before I knew how strong were your objections to help from me. Nobody knows this but myself. Even Mr Dodd thinks my father advanced the money. The ten dollars the rascal would have kept, but I made him disgorge it. I did it all while you were looking for the letter in the woods. Pray forget all about it, and any pain you may have had from J. M."

Frank and practical as this letter appeared to be, and, doubtless, as it was intended to be by its writer, the reader will not fail to notice that Miss Mayfield said nothing of having overheard Jeff's quarrel with the deputy, and left him to infer that that functionary had betrayed him. It was simply one of those unpleasant details not affecting the result, usually overlooked in feminine ethics.

For a moment Jeff sat pale and dumb, crushed under the ruins of his pride and self-love. For a moment he hated Miss Mayfield, small and triumphant! How she must have inwardly laughed at his speech that morning! With what refined cruelty she had saved this evidence of his humiliation, to work her vengeance on him now. He could not stand it! He could not live under it! He would go back and sell the house—his clothes—everything—to pay this wicked, heartless, cruel girl, that was killing—yes, killing—

A strong hand took the swinging-lantern from his unsteady fingers, a strong hand possessed itself of the papers and Miss Mayfield's note, a strong arm was drawn around him,—for his figure was swaying to and fro, his head was giddy, and his hat had fallen off,—and a strong voice, albeit a little husky, whispered in his ear,—

"Easy, boy! easy on the down grade. It'll be all one in a minit."

Jeff tried to comprehend him, but his brain was whirling.

"Pull yourself together, Jeff!" said Bill, after a pause. "Thar! Look yar!" he said suddenly. "Do you think you can drive SIX?"

The words recalled Jeff to his senses. Bill laid the six reins in his hands. A sense of life, of activity, of POWER, came back to the young man, as his fingers closed deliciously on the far-reaching, thrilling, living leathern sinews that controlled the six horses, and seemed to be instinct and magnetic with their bounding life. Jeff, leaning back against them, felt the strong youthful tide rush back to his heart, and was himself again. Bill, meantime, took the lamp, examined the papers, and read Miss Mayfield's note. A grim smile stole over his face. After a pause, he said again, "Give Blue Grass her head, Jeff. D—n it, she ain't Miss Mayfield!"

Jeff relaxed the muscles of his wrists, so as to throw the thumb and forefingers a trifle forward. This simple action relieved Blue Grass, alias Miss Mayfield, and made the coach steadier and less jerky. Wonderful co-relation of forces.

Bret Harte

"Thar!" said Yuba Bill, quietly putting the coach lamp back in its place; "you're better already. Thar's nothing like six horses to draw a woman out of a man. I've knowed a case where it took eight mustangs, but it was a mulatter from New Orleans, and they are pizen! Ye might hit up a little on the Pinto hoss—he ain't harmin' ye. So! Now, Jeff, take your time, and take it easy, and what's all this yer about?"

To control six fiery mustangs, and at the same time give picturesque and affecting exposition of the subtle struggles of Love and Pride, was a performance beyond Jeff's powers. He had recourse to an angry staccato, which somehow seemed to him as ineffective as his previous discourse to Miss Mayfield; he was a little incoherent, and perhaps mixed his impressions with his facts, but he nevertheless managed to convey to Bill some general idea of the events of the past three days.

"And she sent ye off after that letter, that wasn't thar, while she fixed things up with Dodd?"

"Yes," said Jeff furiously.

"Ye needn't bully the Pinto colt, Jeff; he is doin' his level best. And she snaked that ar ten dollars outer Dodd?"

"Yes; and sent it back to ME. To ME, Bill! At such a time as this! As if I was dead broke!—a mere tramp. As if—"

"In course! in course!" said Bill soothingly, yet turning his head aside to bestow a deceitful smile upon the trees that whirled beside them. "And ye told her ye didn't want her money?"

"Yes, Bill—but it—it—it was AFTER she had done this!"

"Surely! I'll take the lines now, Jeff."

He took them. Jeff relapsed into gloomy silence. The star-light of that dewless Sierran night was bright and cold and passionless. There was no moon to lead the fancy astray with its faint mysteries and suggestions; nothing but a clear, grayish-blue twilight, with sharply silhouetted shadows, pointed here and there with bright large-spaced constant stars. The deep breath of the pine-woods, the faint, cool resinous spices of bay and laurel, at last brought surcease to his wounded spirit. The blessed weariness of exhausted youth stole tenderly on him. His head nodded, dropped. Yuba Bill, with a grim smile, drew him to his side, enveloped him in his blanket, and felt his head at last sink upon his own broad shoulder.

A few minutes later the coach drew up at the "Summit House." Yuba Bill did not dismount, an unusual and distur-bing circumstance that brought the bar-keeper to the veranda.

"What's up, old man?"

"I am."

"Sworn off your reg'lar pizen?"

"My physician," said Bill gravely, "hez ordered me dry champagne every three hours."

Nevertheless, the bar-keeper lingered.

"Who's that you're dry-nussin' up there?"

I regret that I may not give Yuba Bill's literal reply. It sugge-sted a form of inquiry at once distant, indirect, outrageous, and impossible.

The bar-keeper flashed a lantern upon Jeff's curls and his drooping eyelashes and mustaches.

"It's that son o' Briggs o' Tuolumne—pooty boy, ain't he?"

Bill disdained a reply.

"Played himself out down there, I reckon. Left his rifle here in pawn."

"Young man," said Bill gravely.

"Old man."

"Ef you're looking for a safe investment ez will pay ye better than forty-rod whiskey at two bits a glass, jist you hang onter that ar rifle. It may make your fortin yet, or save ye from a drunkard's grave." With this ungracious pleasantry he hurried his dilatory passengers back into the coach, cracked his whip, and was again upon the road. The lights of the "Summit House" presently dropped here and there into the wasting shadows of the trees. Another stretch through the close-set ranks of pines, another dash through the opening, another whirl and rattle by overhanging rocks, and the vehicle was swiftly descending. Bill put his foot on the brake, threw his reins loosely on the necks of his cattle, and looked leisurely back. The great mountain was slowly and steadily rising between them and the valley they quitted.

And at that same moment Miss Mayfield had crept from her bed, and, with a shawl around her pretty little figure, was pressing her eyes against a blank window of the "Half-way House," and wondering where HE was now.

V

The "opening" suggested by Bill was not a fortunate one. Possibly views of business openings in the public-house line taken from the tops of stage-coaches are not as judicious as those taken from less exalted levels. Certain it is that the "goodwill" of the "Lone Star House" promised little more pecuniary value than a conventional blessing. It was in an older and more thickly settled locality than the "Half-way House;" indeed, it was but half a mile away from Campville, famous in '49—a place with a history and a disaster. But young communities are impatient of settlements that through any accident fail to fulfil the extravagant promise of their youth, and the wounded hamlet of Campville had crept into the woods and died. The "Lone Star House" was an attempt to woo the passing travelers from another point; but its road led to Campville, and was already touched by its dry-rot. Bill, who honestly conceived that the infusion of fresh young blood like Jeff's into the stagnant current would quicken it, had to confess his disappointment. "I thought ye could put some go into the shanty, Jeff," said Bill, "and make it lively and invitin'!" But the lack of vitality was not in the landlord, but in the guests. The regular customers were disappointed, vacant, hopeless men, who gathered listlessly on the veranda, and talked vaguely of the past. Their hollow-eyed, feeble impotency affected the stranger, even as it checked all ambition among themselves. Do what Jeff might, the habits

Bret Harte

of the locality were stronger than his individuality; the dead ghosts of the past Campville held their property by invisible mortmain.

In the midst of this struggle the "Half-way House" was sold. Spite of Bill's prediction, the proceeds barely paid Jeff's debts. Aunt Sally prevented any troublesome consideration of HER future, by applying a small surplus of profit to the expenses of a journey back to her relatives in Kentucky. She wrote Jeff a letter of cheerless instruction, reminded him of the fulfillment of her worst prophecies regarding him, but begged him, in her absence, to rely solely upon the "Word." "For the sperrit killeth," she added vaguely. Whether this referred figuratively to Jeff's business, he did not stop to consider. He was more interested in the information that the Mayfields had removed to the "Summit Hotel" two days after he had left. "She allowed it was for her health's sake," continued Aunt Sally, "but I reckon it's another name for one of them city fellers who j'ined their party and is keepin' company with her now. They talk o' property and stocks and sich worldly trifles all the time, and it's easy to see their idees is set together. It's allowed at the Forks that Mr. Mayfield paid Parker's bill for you. I said it wasn't so, fur ye'd hev told me; but if it is so, Jeff, and ye didn't tell me, it was for only one puppos, and that wos that Mayfield bribed ye to break off with his darter! That was WHY you went off so suddent, 'like a thief in the night,' and why Miss Mayfield never let on a word about you after you left—not even your name!"

Jeff crushed the letter between his fingers, and, going behind the bar, poured out half a glass of stimulant and drank it. It was not the first time since he came to the "Lone Star House" that he had found this easy relief from his present thought; it was not the first time that he had found this dangerous ally of sure and swift service in bringing him up or down to that level of his dreary, sodden guests, so necessary to his trade.

Jeff had not the excuse of the inborn drunkard's taste. He was impulsive and extreme. At the end of the four weeks he came out on the porch one night as Bill drew up. "You must take me from this place to-night," he said, in a broken voice scarce like his own. "When we're on the road we can arrange matters, but I must go to-night."

"But where?" asked Bill.

"Anywhere! Only I must go from here. I shall go if I have to walk."

Bill looked hard at the young man. His face was flushed, his eyes blood-shot, and his hands trembled, not with excitement, but with a vacant, purposeless impotence. Bill looked a little relieved. "You've been drinking too hard. Jeff, I thought better of ye than that!"

"I think better of MYSELF than that," said Jeff, with a certain wild, half-hysterical laugh, "and that is why I want to go. Don't be alarmed, Bill," he added; "I have strength enough to save myself, and I shall! But it isn't worth the struggle HERE."

He left the "Lone Star House" that night. He would, he said to Bill, go on to Sacramento, and try to get a situation as clerk or porter there; he was too old to learn a trade. He said little more. When, after forty-eight hours' inability to eat, drink, or sleep, Bill, looking at his haggard face and staring eyes, pressed him to partake, medicinally, from a certain black bottle, Jeff gently put it aside, and saying, with a sad smile, "I can get along without it; I've gone through more than this," left his mentor in a state of mingled admiration and perplexity.

At Sacramento he found a commercial "opening." But

certain habits of personal independence, combined with a direct truthfulness and simplicity, were not conducive to business advancement. He was frank, and in his habits impulsive and selfishly outspoken. His employer, a good-natured man, successful in his way, anxious to serve his own interest and Jeff's equally, strove and labored with him, but in vain. His employer's wife, a still more good-natured woman, successful in her way, and equally anxious to serve Jeff's interests and her own, also strove with him as unsuccessfully. At the end of a month he discharged his employer, after a simple, boyish, utterly unbusiness-like interview, and secretly tore up his wife's letter. "I don't know what to make of that chap," said the husband to his wife; "he's about as civilized as an Injun." "And as conceited," added the lady.

Howbeit he took his conceit, his sorrows, his curls, mustaches, broad shoulders, and fifty dollars into humble lodgings in a back street. The days succeeding this were the most restful he had passed since he left the "Half-way House." To wander through the town, half conscious of its strangeness and novel bustling life, and to dream of a higher and nobler future with Miss Mayfield—to feel no responsibility but that of waiting—was, I regret to say, a pleasure to him. He made no acquaintances except among the poorer people and the children. He was sometimes hungry, he was always poorly clad, but these facts carried no degradation with them now. He read much, and in his way—Jeff's way—tried to improve his mind; his recent commercial experience had shown him various infelicities in his speech and accent. He learned to correct certain provincialisms. He was conscious that Miss Mayfield must have noticed them, yet his odd irrational pride kept him from ever regretting them, if they had offered a possible excuse for her treatment of him.

On one of these nights his steps chanced to lead him into a

gambling-saloon. The place had offered no temptation to him; his dealings with the goddess Chance had been of less active nature. Nevertheless he placed his last five dollars on the turn of a card. He won. He won repeatedly; his gains had reached a considerable sum when, flushed, excited, and absorbed, he was suddenly conscious that he had become the centre of observation at the table. Looking up, he saw that the dealer had paused, and, with the cards in his motionless fingers, was gazing at him with fixed eyes and a white face.

Jeff rose and passed hurriedly to his side. "What's the matter?"

The gambler shrunk slightly as he approached. "What's your name?"

"Briggs."

"God! I knew it! How much have you got there?" he continued, in a quick whisper, pointing to Jeff's winnings.

"Five hundred dollars."

"I'll give you double if you'll get up and quit the board!"

"Why?" asked Jeff haughtily.

"Why?" repeated the man fiercely; "why? Well, your father shot himself thar, where you're sittin', at this table;" and he added, with a half-forced, half-hysterical laugh, "HE'S PLAYIN' AT ME OVER YOUR SHOULDERS!"

Jeff lifted a face as colorless as the gambler's own, went back to his seat, and placed his entire gains on a single card. The gambler looked at him nervously, but dealt. There was a pause, a slight movement where Jeff stood, and then a simultaneous cry from the players as they turned towards him. But his seat was vacant. "Run after him! Call him back! HE'S WON AGAIN!" But he had vanished utterly.

HOW he left, or what indeed followed, he never clearly remembered. His movements must have been automatic, for when, two hours later, he found himself at the "Pioneer" coach office, with his carpet-bag and blankets by his side, he could not recall how or why he had come! He had a dumb impression that he had barely escaped some dire calamity,— rather that he had only temporarily averted it,—and that he was still in the shadow of some impending catastrophe of destiny. He must go somewhere, he must do something to be saved! He had no money, he had no friends; even Yuba Bill had been transferred to another route, miles away. Yet, in the midst of this stupefaction, it was a part of his strange mental condition that trivial details of Miss Mayfield's face and figure, and even apparel, were constantly before him, to the exclusion of consecutive thought. A collar she used to wear, a ribbon she had once tied around her waist, a blue vein in her dropped eyelid, a curve in her soft, full, bird-like throat, the arch of her in-step in her small boots—all these were plainer to him than the future, or even the present. But a voice in his ear, a figure before his abstracted eyes, at last broke upon his reverie.

"Jeff Briggs!"

Jeff mechanically took the outstretched hand of a young clerk of the Pioneer Coach Company, who had once accompanied Yuba Bill and stopped at the "Half-way House." He endeavored to collect his thoughts; here seemed to be an opportunity to go somewhere!

"What are you doing now?" said the young man briskly.

"Nothing," said Jeff simply.

"Oh, I see—going home!"

Home! the word stung sharply through Jeff's benumbed consciousness.

"No," he stammered, "that is—"

"Look here, Jeff," broke in the young man, "I've got a chance for you that don't fall in a man's way every day. Wells, Fargo & Co.'s treasure messenger from Robinson's Ferry to Mempheys has slipped out. The place is vacant. I reckon I can get it for you."

"When?"

"Now—to-night."

"I'm ready."

"Come, then."

In ten minutes they were in the company's office, where its manager, a man famous in those days for his boldness and shrewdness, still lingered in the dispatch of business.

The young clerk briefly but deferentially stated certain facts. A few questions and answers followed, of which Jeff heard only the words "Tuolumne" and "Yuba Bill."

"Sit down, Mr. Briggs. Good-night, Roberts."

The young clerk, with an encouraging smile at Jeff, bowed himself out as the manager seated himself at his desk and began to write.

"You know the country pretty well between the Fork and the Summit, Mr. Briggs?" he said, without looking up.

"I lived there," said Jeff.

"That was some months ago, wasn't it?"

"Six months," said Jeff, with a sigh.

"It's changed for the worse since your house was shut up. There's a long stretch of unsettled country infested by bad characters."

Jeff sat silent. "Briggs."

"Sir?"

"The last man but one who preceded you was shot by road agents."*

    * Highway robbers.

"Yes, sir."

"We lost sixty thousand dollars up there."

"Yes?"

"Your father was Briggs of Tuolumne?"

"Yes, sir." Jeff's head dropped, but, glancing shyly up, he saw a pleasant smile on his questioner's face. He was still writing rapidly, but was apparently enjoying at the same time some pleasant recollection.

"Your father and I lost nearly sixty thousand dollars together one night, ten years ago, when we were both younger."

"Yes, sir," said Jeff dubiously.

"But it was OUR OWN MONEY, Jeff."

"Yes, sir."

"Here's your appointment," he said briefly, throwing away his pen, folding what he had written, and handing it to Jeff. It was the first time that he had looked at him since he entered. He now held out his hand, grasped Jeff's, and said, "Good-night!"

VI

It was late the next evening when Jeff drew up at the coach office at Robinson's Ferry, where he was to await the coming of the Summit coach. His mind, lifted only temporarily out of its denumbed condition during his interview with the manager, again fell back into its dull abstraction. Fully embarked upon his dangerous journey, accepting all the meaning of the trust imposed upon him, he was yet vaguely conscious that he did not realize its full importance. He had neither the dread nor the stimulation of coming danger. He had faced death before in the boyish confidence of animal spirits; his pulse now was scarcely stirred with anticipation. Once or twice before, in the extravagance of his passion, he had imagined himself rescuing Miss Mayfield from danger, or even dying for her. During his journey his mind had dwelt fully and minutely on every detail of their brief acquaintance; she was continually before him, the tones of her voice were in his ears, the suggestive touch of her fingers, the thrill that his lips had felt when he kissed them—all were with him now, but only as a memory. In his coming fate, in his future life, he saw her not. He believed it was a premonition of coming death.

He made a few preparations. The company's agent had told him that the treasure, letters, and dispatches, which had accumulated to a considerable amount, would be handed to him on the box; and that the arms and ammunition were in the boot. A less courageous and determined man might have been affected by the cold, practical brutality of certain advice and instructions offered him by the agent, but Jeff recognized this compliment to his determination, even before the agent concluded his speech by saying, "But I reckon they knew what they were about in the lower office when they sent YOU up. I dare say you kin give me p'ints, ef ye cared to, for all ye're soft spoken. There are only four passengers booked through; we hev to be a little partikler, suspectin' spies! Two of the four ye kin depend upon to get the top o' their d—d heads blowed off the first fire," he added grimly.

At ten o'clock the Summit coach flashed, rattled, glittered, and snapped, like a disorganized firework, up to the door of the company's office. A familiar figure, but more than usually truculent and aggressive, slowly descended with violent oaths from the box. Without seeing Jeff, it strode into the office.

"Now then," said Yuba Bill, addressing the agent, "whar's that God-forsaken fool that Wells, Fargo & Co. hev sent up yar to take charge o' their treasure? Because I'd like to introduce him to the champion idgit of Calaveras County, that's been selected to go to h-ll with him; and that's me, Yuba Bill! P'int him out. Don't keep me waitin'!"

The agent grinned and pointed to Jeff.

Both men recoiled in astonishment. Yuba Bill was the first to recover his speech.

"It's a lie!" he roared; "or somebody has been putting up a job on ye, Jeff! Because I've been twenty years in the service, and am such a nat'ral born mule that when the company strokes my back and sez, 'You're the on'y mule we kin trust, Bill,' I starts up and goes out as a blasted wooden figgerhead for road agents to lay fur and practice on, it don't follow that YOU'VE any call to go."

"It was my own seeking, Bill," said Jeff, with one of his old, sweet, boyish smiles. "I didn't know YOU were to drive. But you're not going back on me now, Bill, are you? you're not going to send me off with another volunteer?"

"That be d—d!" growled Bill. Nevertheless, for ten minutes he reviled the Pioneer Coach Company with picturesque imprecation, tendered his resignation repeatedly to the agent, and at the end of that time, as everybody expected, mounted the box, and with a final malediction, involving the whole settlement, was off.

On the road, Jeff, in a few hurried sentences, told his story. Bill scarcely seemed to listen. "Look yar, Jeff," he said suddenly.

"Yes, Bill."

"If the worst happens, and ye go under, you'll tell your father, IF I DON'T HAPPEN TO SEE HIM FIRST, it wasn't no job of mine, and I did my best to get ye out of it."

"Yes," said Jeff, in a faint voice.

"It mayn't be so bad," said Bill, softening; "they KNOW, d—n 'em, we've got a pile aboard, ez well as if they seed that agent gin it ye, but they also know we've pre-pared!"

"I wasn't thinking of that, Bill; I was thinking of my father." And he told Bill of the gambling episode at Sacramento.

"D'ye mean to say ye left them hounds with a thousand

dollars of yer hard-earned—"

"Gambling gains, Bill," interrupted Jeff quietly.

"Exactly! Well!" Bill subsided into an incoherent growl. After a few moments' pause, he began again. "Yer ready as ye used to be with a six-shooter, Jeff, time's when ye was a boy, and I uster chuck half-dollars in the air fur ye to make warts on?"

"I reckon," said Jeff, with a faint smile.

"Thar's two p'ints on the road to be looked to: the woods beyond the blacksmith's shop that uster be; the fringe of alder and buckeye by the crossing below your house—p'ints where they kin fetch you without a show. Thar's two ways o' meetin' them thar. One way ez to pull up and trust to luck and brag. The other way is to whip up and yell, and send the whole six kiting by like h-ll!"

"Yes," said Jeff.

"The only drawback to that plan is this: the road lies along the edge of a precipice, straight down a thousand feet into the river. Ef these devils get a shot into any one o' the six and it DROPS, the coach turns sharp off, and down we go, the whole kerboodle of us, plump into the Stanislaus!"

"AND THEY DON'T GET THE MONEY," said Jeff quietly.

"Well, no!" replied Yuba Bill, staring at Jeff, whose face was set as a flint against the darkness. "I should reckon not." He then drew a long breath, glanced at Jeff again, and said between his teeth, "Well, I'm d—d!"

At the next station they changed horses, Bill personally

supervising, especially as regarded the welfare and proper condition of Blue Grass, who here was brought out as a leader. Formerly there was no change of horses at this station, and this novelty excited Jeff's remark. "These yar chaps say thar's no station at the Summit now," growled Bill, in explanation; "the hotel is closed, and it's all private property, bought by some chap from 'Frisco. Thar ought to be a law agin such doin's!"

This suggested obliteration of the last traces of Miss Mayfield seemed to Jeff as only a corroboration of his premonition. He should never hear from her again! Yet to have stood under the roof that last sheltered her; to, perchance, have met some one who had seen her later—this was a fancy that had haunted him on his journey. It was all over now. Perhaps it was for the best.

With the sinking behind of the lights of the station, the occupants of the coach knew that the dangerous part of the journey had begun. The two guards in the coach had already made obtrusive and warlike preparations, to the ill-concealed disgust of Yuba Bill "I d hev been willin' to get through this yar job without the burnin' of powder, but ef any of them devils ez is waitin' for us would be content with a shot at them fancy policemen inside, I'd pull up and give 'em a show!" Having relieved his mind, Bill said no more, and the two men relapsed into silence. The moon shone brightly and peacefully, a fact pointed out by Bill as unfavorably deepening the shadows of the woods, and bringing the coach and the road into greater relief.

An hour passed. What were Yuba Bill's thoughts are not a part of this history; that they were turbulent and aggressive might be inferred from the occasional growls and interjected oaths that broke from his lips. But Jeff, strange anomaly, due perhaps to youth and moonlight, was wrapped in a sensuous dream of Miss Mayfield, of the scent of her dark hair as he had drawn her to his side, of the outlines of her sweet form, that had for a moment lightly touched his own—of anything, I fear, but the death he believed he was hastening to. But—

"Jeff," said Bill, in an unmistakable tone.

"Yes," said Jeff.

"THAT AR CLUMP O' BUCKEYE ON THE RIDGE! Ready there!" (Leaning over the box, to the guards within.) A responsive rustle in the coach, which now bounded forward as if instinct with life and intelligence.

"Jeff," said Bill, in an odd, altered voice, "take the lines a minit." Jeff took them. Bill stooped towards the boot. A peaceful moment! A peaceful outlook from the coach; the white moonlit road stretching to the ridge, no noise but the steady gallop of the horses!

Then a yellow flash, breaking from the darkness of the buckeye; a crack like the snap of a whip; Yuba Bill steadying himself for a moment, and then dropping at Jeff's feet!

"They got me, Jeff! But—I DRAWED THEIR FIRE! Don't drop the lines! Don't speak! For—they—think I'm YOU and you ME!"

The flash had illuminated Jeff as to the danger, as to Bill's sacrifice, but above all, and overwhelming all, to a thrilling sense of his own power and ability.

Yet he sat like a statue. Six masked figures had appeared from the very ground, clinging to the bits of the horses. The coach stopped. Two wild purposeless shots—the first and last fired by the guards—were answered by the muzzle of six

Bret Harte

rifles pointed into the windows, and the passengers foolishly and impotently filed out into the road.

"Now, Bill," said a voice, which Jeff instantly recognized as the blacksmith's, "we won't keep ye long. So hand down the treasure."

The man's foot was on the wheel; in another instant he would be beside Jeff, and discovery was certain. Jeff leaned over and unhooked the coach lamp, as if to assist him with its light. As if in turning, he STUMBLED, broke the lamp, ignited the kerosene, and scattered the wick and blazing fluid over the haunches of the wheelers! The maddened animals gave one wild plunge forwards, the coach followed twice its length, throwing the blacksmith under its wheels, and driving the other horses towards the bank. But as the lamp broke in Jeff's right hand, his practiced left hand discharged its hidden Derringer at the head of the robber who had held the bit of Blue Grass, and, throwing the useless weapon away, he laid the whip smartly on her back. She leaped forward madly, dragging the other leaders with her, and in the next moment they were free and wildly careering down the grade.

A dozen shots followed them. The men were protected by the coach, but Yuba Bill groaned.

"Are you hit again?" asked Jeff hastily. He had forgotten his saviour.

"No; but the horses are! I felt 'em! Look at 'em, Jeff."

Jeff had gathered up the almost useless reins. The horses were running away; but Blue Grass was limping.

"For God's sake," said Bill, desperately dragging his wounded figure above the dash-board, "keep her up! LIFT

HER UP, Jeff, till we pass the curve. Don't let her drop, or we're—"

"Can you hold the reins?" said Jeff quickly.

"Give 'em here!"

Jeff passed them to the wounded man. Then, with his bowie-knife between his teeth, he leaped over the dash-board on the backs of the wheelers. He extinguished the blazing drops that the wind had not blown out of their smarting haunches, and with the skill and instinct of a Mexican vaquero, made his way over their turbulent tossing backs to Blue Grass, cut her traces and reins, and as the vehicle neared the curve, with a sharp lash, drove her to the bank, where she sank even as the coach darted by. Bill uttered a feeble "Hurrah!" but at the same moment the reins dropped from his fingers, and he sank at the bottom of the boot.

Riding postilion-wise, Jeff could control the horses. The dangerous curve was passed, but not the possibility of pursuit. The single leader he was bestriding was panting— more than that, he was SWEATING, and from the evidence of Jeff's hands, sweating BLOOD! Back of his shoulder was a jagged hole, from which his life-blood was welling. The off-wheel horse was limping too. That last volley was no foolish outburst of useless rage, but was deliberate and premeditated skill. Jeff drew the reins, and as the coach stopped, the horse he was riding fell dead. Into the silence that followed broke the measured beat of horses' hoofs on the road above. He was pursued!

To select the best horse of the remaining unscathed three, to break open the boot and place the treasure on his back, and to abandon and leave the senseless Bill lying there, was the unhesitating work of a moment. Great heroes and great

Bret Harte

lovers are invariably one-ideaed men, and Jeff was at that moment both.

Eighty thousand dollars in gold-dust and Jeff's weight was a handicap. Nevertheless he flew forward like the wind. Presently he fell to listening. A certain hoof-beat in the rear was growing more distinct. A bitter thought flashed through his mind. He looked back. Over the hill appeared the foremost of his pursuers. It was the blacksmith, mounted on the fleetest horse in the county—Jeff's OWN horse—Rabbit!

But there are compensations in all new trials. As Jeff faced round again, he saw he had reached the open table-land, and the bleak walls and ghastly, untenanted windows of the "Half-way House" rose before him in the distance. Jeff was master of the ground here! He was entering the shadow of the woods—Miss Mayfield's woods! and there was a cut off from the road, and a bridle-path, known only to himself, hard by. To find it, leap the roadside ditch, dash through the thicket, and rein up by the road again, was swiftly done.

Take a gentle woman, betray her trust, outrage her best feelings, drive her into a corner, and you have a fury! Take a gentle, trustful man, abuse him, show him the folly of this gentleness and kindness, prove to him that it is weakness, drive him into a corner, and you have a savage! And it was this savage, with an Indian's memory, and an Indian's eye and ear, that suddenly confronted the blacksmith.

What more! A single shot from a trained hand and one-ideaed intellect settled the blacksmith's business, and temporarily ended this Iliad! I say temporarily, for Mr. Dodd, formerly deputy-sheriff, prudently pulled up at the top of the hill, and observing his principal bend his head forwards and act like a drunken man, until he reeled, limp and sideways, from the saddle, and noticing further that Jeff took his place with a well-filled saddle-bag, concluded to follow cautiously and unobtrusively in the rear.

VII

But Jeff saw him not. With mind and will bent on one object—to reach the first habitation, the "Summit," and send back help and assistance to his wounded comrade—he urged Rabbit forward. The mare knew her rider, but he had no time for caresses. Through the smarting of his hands he had only just noticed that they were badly burned, and the skin was peeling from them; he had confounded the blood that was flowing from a cut on his scalp, with that from the wounded horse. It was one hour yet to the "Summit," but the road was good, the moon was bright, he knew what Rabbit could do, and it was not yet ten o'clock.

As the white outbuildings and irregular outlines of the "Summit House" began to be visible, Jeff felt a singular return of his former dreamy abstraction. The hour of peril, anger, and excitement he had just passed through seemed something of years ago, or rather to be obliterated with all else that had passed since he had looked upon that scene. Yet it was all changed—strangely changed! What Jeff had taken for the white, wooden barns and outhouses were greenhouses and conservatories. The "Summit Hotel" was a picturesque villa, nestling in the self-same trees, but approached through cultivated fields, dwellings of laborers, parklike gates and walls, and all the bountiful appointments of wealth and security. Jeff thought of Yuba Bill's malediction, and understood it as he gazed.

The barking of dogs announced his near approach to the principal entrance. Lights were still burning in the upper windows of the house and its offices. He was at once surrounded by the strange medley of a Californian ranchero's service, peons, Chinese, and vaqueros. Jeff briefly stated his business. "Ah, Carrajo!" This was a matter for the major-domo, or, better, the padrone—Wilson! But the padrone, Wilson, called out by the tumult, appeared in person—a handsome, resolute, middle-aged man, who, in a twinkling, dispersed the group to barn and stable with a dozen orders of preparation, and then turned to Jeff.

"You are hurt; come in."

Jeff followed him dazedly into the house. The same sense of remote abstraction, of vague dreaminess, was overcoming him. He resented it, and fought against it, but in vain; he was only half conscious that his host had bathed his head and given him some slight restorative, had said something to him soothingly, and had left him. Jeff wondered if he had fainted, or was about to faint,—he had a nervous dread of that womanish weakness,—or if he were really hurt worse than he believed. He tried to master himself and grasp the situation by minutely examining the room. It was luxuriously furnished; Jeff had but once before sat in such an arm-chair as the one that half embraced him, and as a boy he had dim recollections of a life like this, of which his father was part. To poor Jeff, with his throbbing head, his smarting hands, and his lapsing moments of half forgetfulness, this seemed to be a return of his old premonition. There was a vague perfume in the room, like that which he remembered when he was in the woods with Miss Mayfield. He believed he was growing faint again, and was about to rise, when the door opened behind him.

Bret Harte

"Is there anything we can do for you? Mr. Wilson has gone to seek your friend, and has sent Manuel for a doctor."

HER voice! He rose hurriedly, turned; SHE was standing in the doorway!

She uttered a slight cry, turned very pale, advanced towards him, stopped and leaned against the chimney-piece.

"I didn't know it was YOU."

With her actual presence Jeff's dream and weakness fled. He rose up before her, his old bashful, stammering, awkward self.

"I didn't know YOU lived here, Miss Mayfield."

"If you had sent word you were coming," said Miss Mayfield, recovering her color brightly in one cheek.

The possibility of having sent a messenger in advance to advise Miss Mayfield of his projected visit did not strike Jeff as ridiculous. Your true lover is far beyond such trivialities. He accepted the rebuke meekly. He said he was sorry.

"You might have known it."

"What, Miss Mayfield?"

"That I was here, if you WISHED to know."

Jeff did not reply. He bowed his head and clasped his burned hands together. Miss Mayfield saw their raw surfaces, saw the ugly cut on his head, pitied him, but went on hastily, with both cheeks burning, to say, womanlike, what was then deepest in her heart:

"My brother-in-law told me your adventure; but I did not know until I entered this room that the gentleman I wished to help was one who had once rejected my assistance, who had misunderstood me, and cruelly insulted me! Oh, forgive me, Mr. Briggs" (Jeff had risen). "I did not mean THAT. But, Mr. Jeff—Jeff—oh!" (She had caught his tortured hand and had wrung a movement of pain from him.) "Oh, dear! what did I do now? But Mr. Jeff, after what has passed, after what you said to me when you went away, when you were at that dreadful place, Campville, when you were two months in Sacramento, you might—YOU OUGHT TO HAVE LET ME KNOW IT!"

Jeff turned. Her face, more beautiful than he had ever seen it, alive and eloquent with every thought that her woman's speech but half expressed, was very near his—so near, that under her honest eyes the wretched scales fell from his own, his self-wrought shackles crumbled away, and he dropped upon his knees at her feet as she sank into the chair he had quitted. Both his hands were grasped in her own.

"YOU went away, and I STAYED," she said reflectively.

"I had no home, Miss Mayfield."

"Nor had I. I had to buy this," she said, with a delicious simplicity; "and bring a family here too," she added, "in case YOU"—she stopped, with a slight color.

"Forgive me," said Jeff, burying his face in her hands.

"Jeff."

"Jessie."

"Don't you think you were a LITTLE—just a little—mean?"

"Yes."

Miss Mayfield uttered a faint sigh. He looked into her anxious cheeks and eyes, his arm stole round her; their lips met for the first time in one long lingering kiss. Then, I fear, for the second time.

"Jeff," said Miss Mayfield, suddenly becoming practical and sweetly possessory, "you must have your hands bound up in cotton."

"Yes," said Jeff cheerfully.

"And you must go instantly to bed."

Jeff stared.

"Because my sister will think it very late for me to be sitting up with a gentleman."

The idea that Miss Mayfield was responsible to anybody was something new to Jeff. But he said hastily, "I must stay and wait for Bill. He risked his life for me."

"Oh, yes! You must tell me all about it. I may wait for THAT!"

Jeff possessed himself of the chair; in some way he also possessed himself of Miss Mayfield without entirely dispossessing her. Then he told his story. He hesitated over the episode of the blacksmith. "I'm afraid I killed him, Jessie."

Miss Mayfield betrayed little concern at this possible extreme measure with a dangerous neighbor. "He cut your head, Jeff," she said, passing her little hand through his curls.

"No," said Jeff hastily, "that must have been done BEFORE."

"Well," said Miss Mayfield conclusively, "he would if he'd dared. And you brought off that wretched money in spite of him. Poor dear Jeff."

"Yes," said Jeff, kissing her.

"Where is it?" asked Jessie, looking round the room.

"Oh, just out there!"

"Out where?"

"On my horse, you know, outside the door," continued Jeff, a little uneasily, as he rose. "I'll go and—"

"You careless boy," said Miss Mayfield, jumping up, "I'll go with you."

They passed out on the porch together, holding each other's hands, like children. The forgotten Rabbit was not there. Miss Mayfield called a vaquero.

"Ah, yes!—the caballero's horse. Of a certainty the other caballero had taken it!"

"The other caballero!" gasped Jeff.

"Si, senor. The one who arrived with you, or a moment, the very next moment, after you. 'Your friend,' he said."

Jeff staggered against the porch, and cast one despairing reproachful look at Miss Mayfield.

"Oh, Jeff! Jeff! don't look so. I know I ought not to have kept you! It's a mistake, Jeff, believe me."

"It's no mistake," said Jeff hoarsely. "Go!" he said, turning to the vaquero, "go!—bring—" But his speech failed. He attempted to gesticulate with his hands, ran forward a few steps, staggered, and fell fainting on the ground.

"Help me with the caballero into the blue room," said Miss Mayfield, white as Jeff. "And hark ye, Manuel! You know every ruffian, man or woman, on this road. That horse and those saddle-bags must be here to-morrow, if you have to pay DOUBLE WHAT THEY'RE WORTH!"

"Si, senora."

Jeff went off into fever, into delirium, into helpless stupor. From time to time he moaned "Bill" and "the treasure." On the third day, in a lucid interval, as he lay staring at the wall, Miss Mayfield put in his hand a letter from the company, acknowledging the receipt of the treasure, thanking him for his zeal, and inclosing a handsome check.

Jeff sat up, and put his hands to his head.

"I told you it was taken by mistake, and was easily found,' said Miss Mayfield, "didn't I?"

"Yes,—and Bill?"

"You know he is so much better that he expects to leave us next week."

"And—Jessie!"

"There—go to sleep!"

At the end of a week she introduced Jeff to her sister-in-law, having previously run her fingers through his hair to insure that becomingness to his curls which would better indicate his moral character; and spoke of him as one of her oldest Californian friends.

At the end of two weeks she again presented him as her affianced husband—a long engagement of a year being just passed. Mr. Wilson, who was bored by the mountain life, undertaken to please his rich wife and richer sister, saw a chance of escape here, and bore willing testimony to the distant Mr. and Mrs. Mayfield of the excellence of Miss Jessie's choice. And Yuba Bill was Jeff's best man.

The name of Briggs remained a power in Tuolumne and Calaveras County. Mr. and Mrs. Briggs never had but one word of disagreement or discussion. One day, Jeff, looking over some old accounts of his wife's, found an unreceipted, unvouched for expenditure of twenty thousand dollars. "What is this for, Jessie?" he asked.

"Oh, it's all right, Jeff!"

But here the now business-like and practical Mr. Briggs, father of a family, felt called upon to make some general remarks regarding the necessity of exactitude in accounts, etc.

"But I'd rather not tell you, Jeff."

"But you ought to, Jessie."

"Well then, dear, it was to get those saddle-bags of yours from that rascal, Dodd," said little Mrs. Briggs meekly.

ABOUT THE AUTHOR

Francis Bret Harte (August 25, 1836–May 6, 1902) was an American author and poet, best remembered for his accounts of pioneering life in California.

Born in Albany, New York, Harte moved to California in 1853, later working there in a number of capacities, including miner, teacher, messenger, and journalist. He spent part of his life in the northern California coast town now known as Arcata, at the time it was just a mining camp on Humboldt Bay.

His first literary efforts, including poetry and prose, appeared in The Californian, an early literary journal edited by Charles Henry Webb. In 1868 he became editor of The Overland Monthly, another new literary magazine, but this one more in tune with the pioneering spirit of excitement in California. His story, "The Luck of Roaring Camp," appeared in the magazine's second edition, propelling Harte to nationwide fame.

As an established literary figure, he was appointed to the position of United States Consul in the town of Krefeld, Germany in 1878 and Glasgow in 1880. In 1885 he settled in London. During the thirty years he spent in Europe, he never abandoned writing, and maintained a prodigious output of stories that retained the freshness of his earlier work. He died in England in 1902.

Choose from Thousands of 1stWorldLibrary Classics By

A. M. Barnard
Ada Leverson
Adolphus William Ward
Aesop
Agatha Christie
Alexander Aaronsohn
Alexander Kielland
Alexandre Dumas
Alfred Gatty
Alfred Ollivant
Alice Duer Miller
Alice Turner Curtis
Alice Dunbar
Allen Chapman
Alleyne Ireland
Ambrose Bierce
Amelia E. Barr
Amory H. Bradford
Andrew Lang
Andrew McFarland Davis
Andy Adams
Angela Brazil
Anna Alice Chapin
Anna Sewell
Annie Besant
Annie Hamilton Donnell
Annie Payson Call
Annie Roe Carr
Annonaymous
Anton Chekhov
Archibald Lee Fletcher
Arnold Bennett
Arthur C. Benson
Arthur Conan Doyle
Arthur M. Winfield
Arthur Ransome
Arthur Schnitzler
Arthur Train
Atticus
B.H. Baden-Powell
B. M. Bower
B. C. Chatterjee
Baroness Emmuska Orczy
Baroness Orczy
Basil King
Bayard Taylor
Ben Macomber
Bertha Muzzy Bower
Bjornstjerne Bjornson

Booth Tarkington
Boyd Cable
Bram Stoker
C. Collodi
C. E. Orr
C. M. Ingleby
Carolyn Wells
Catherine Parr Traill
Charles A. Eastman
Charles Amory Beach
Charles Dickens
Charles Dudley Warner
Charles Farrar Browne
Charles Ives
Charles Kingsley
Charles Klein
Charles Hanson Towne
Charles Lathrop Pack
Charles Romyn Dake
Charles Whibley
Charles Willing Beale
Charlotte M. Braeme
Charlotte M. Yonge
Charlotte Perkins Stetson
Clair W. Hayes
Clarence Day Jr.
Clarence E. Mulford
Clemence Housman
Confucius
Coningsby Dawson
Cornelis DeWitt Wilcox
Cyril Burleigh
D. H. Lawrence
Daniel Defoe
David Garnett
Dinah Craik
Don Carlos Janes
Donald Keyhoe
Dorothy Kilner
Dougan Clark
Douglas Fairbanks
E. Nesbit
E. P. Roe
E. Phillips Oppenheim
E. S. Brooks
Earl Barnes
Edgar Rice Burroughs
Edith Van Dyne
Edith Wharton

Edward Everett Hale
Edward J. O'Biren
Edward S. Ellis
Edwin L. Arnold
Eleanor Atkins
Eleanor Hallowell Abbott
Eliot Gregory
Elizabeth Gaskell
Elizabeth McCracken
Elizabeth Von Arnim
Ellem Key
Emerson Hough
Emilie F. Carlen
Emily Bronte
Emily Dickinson
Enid Bagnold
Enilor Macartney Lane
Erasmus W. Jones
Ernie Howard Pie
Ethel May Dell
Ethel Turner
Ethel Watts Mumford
Eugene Sue
Eugenie Foa
Eugene Wood
Eustace Hale Ball
Evelyn Everett-green
Everard Cotes
F. H. Cheley
F. J. Cross
F. Marion Crawford
Fannie E. Newberry
Federick Austin Ogg
Ferdinand Ossendowski
Fergus Hume
Florence A. Kilpatrick
Fremont B. Deering
Francis Bacon
Francis Darwin
Frances Hodgson Burnett
Frances Parkinson Keyes
Frank Gee Patchin
Frank Harris
Frank Jewett Mather
Frank L. Packard
Frank V. Webster
Frederic Stewart Isham
Frederick Trevor Hill
Frederick Winslow Taylor

Friedrich Kerst
Friedrich Nietzsche
Fyodor Dostoyevsky
G.A. Henty
G.K. Chesterton
Gabrielle E. Jackson
Garrett P. Serviss
Gaston Leroux
George A. Warren
George Ade
Geroge Bernard Shaw
George Cary Eggleston
George Durston
George Ebers
George Eliot
George Gissing
George MacDonald
George Meredith
George Orwell
George Sylvester Viereck
George Tucker
George W. Cable
George Wharton James
Gertrude Atherton
Gordon Casserly
Grace E. King
Grace Gallatin
Grace Greenwood
Grant Allen
Guillermo A. Sherwell
Gulielma Zollinger
Gustav Flaubert
H. A. Cody
H. B. Irving
H.C. Bailey
H. G. Wells
H. H. Munro
H. Irving Hancock
H. R. Naylor
H. Rider Haggard
H. W. C. Davis
Haldeman Julius
Hall Caine
Hamilton Wright Mabie
Hans Christian Andersen
Harold Avery
Harold McGrath
Harriet Beecher Stowe
Harry Castlemon
Harry Coghill
Harry Houidini

Hayden Carruth
Helent Hunt Jackson
Helen Nicolay
Hendrik Conscience
Hendy David Thoreau
Henri Barbusse
Henrik Ibsen
Henry Adams
Henry Ford
Henry Frost
Henry James
Henry Jones Ford
Henry Seton Merriman
Henry W Longfellow
Herbert A. Giles
Herbert Carter
Herbert N. Casson
Herman Hesse
Hildegard G. Frey
Homer
Honore De Balzac
Horace B. Day
Horace Walpole
Horatio Alger Jr.
Howard Pyle
Howard R. Garis
Hugh Lofting
Hugh Walpole
Humphry Ward
Ian Maclaren
Inez Haynes Gillmore
Irving Bacheller
Isabel Cecilia Williams
Isabel Hornibrook
Israel Abrahams
Ivan Turgenev
J.G.Austin
J. Henri Fabre
J. M. Barrie
J. M. Walsh
J. Macdonald Oxley
J. R. Miller
J. S. Fletcher
J. S. Knowles
J. Storer Clouston
J. W. Duffield
Jack London
Jacob Abbott
James Allen
James Andrews
James Baldwin

James Branch Cabell
James DeMille
James Joyce
James Lane Allen
James Lane Allen
James Oliver Curwood
James Oppenheim
James Otis
James R. Driscoll
Jane Abbott
Jane Austen
Jane L. Stewart
Janet Aldridge
Jens Peter Jacobsen
Jerome K. Jerome
Jessie Graham Flower
John Buchan
John Burroughs
John Cournos
John F. Kennedy
John Gay
John Glasworthy
John Habberton
John Joy Bell
John Kendrick Bangs
John Milton
John Philip Sousa
John Taintor Foote
Jonas Lauritz Idemil Lie
Jonathan Swift
Joseph A. Altsheler
Joseph Carey
Joseph Conrad
Joseph E. Badger Jr
Joseph Hergesheimer
Joseph Jacobs
Jules Vernes
Julian Hawthrone
Julie A Lippmann
Justin Huntly McCarthy
Kakuzo Okakura
Karle Wilson Baker
Kate Chopin
Kenneth Grahame
Kenneth McGaffey
Kate Langley Bosher
Kate Langley Bosher
Katherine Cecil Thurston
Katherine Stokes
L. A. Abbot
L. T. Meade

L. Frank Baum
Latta Griswold
Laura Dent Crane
Laura Lee Hope
Laurence Housman
Lawrence Beasley
Leo Tolstoy
Leonid Andreyev
Lewis Carroll
Lewis Sperry Chafer
Lilian Bell
Lloyd Osbourne
Louis Hughes
Louis Joseph Vance
Louis Tracy
Louisa May Alcott
Lucy Fitch Perkins
Lucy Maud Montgomery
Luther Benson
Lydia Miller Middleton
Lyndon Orr
M. Corvus
M. H. Adams
Margaret E. Sangster
Margret Howth
Margaret Vandercook
Margaret W. Hungerford
Margret Penrose
Maria Edgeworth
Maria Thompson Daviess
Mariano Azuela
Marion Polk Angellotti
Mark Overton
Mark Twain
Mary Austin
Mary Catherine Crowley
Mary Cole
Mary Hastings Bradley
Mary Roberts Rinehart
Mary Rowlandson
M. Wollstonecraft Shelley
Maud Lindsay
Max Beerbohm
Myra Kelly
Nathaniel Hawthrone
Nicolo Machiavelli
O. F. Walton
Oscar Wilde

Owen Johnson
P.G. Wodehouse
Paul and Mabel Thorne
Paul G. Tomlinson
Paul Severing
Percy Brebner
Percy Keese Fitzhugh
Peter B. Kyne
Plato
Quincy Allen
R. Derby Holmes
R. L. Stevenson
R. S. Ball
Rabindranath Tagore
Rahul Alvares
Ralph Bonehill
Ralph Henry Barbour
Ralph Victor
Ralph Waldo Emmerson
Rene Descartes
Ray Cummings
Rex Beach
Rex E. Beach
Richard Harding Davis
Richard Jefferies
Richard Le Gallienne
Robert Barr
Robert Frost
Robert Gordon Anderson
Robert L. Drake
Robert Lansing
Robert Lynd
Robert Michael Ballantyne
Robert W. Chambers
Rosa Nouchette Carey
Rudyard Kipling
Saint Augustine
Samuel B. Allison
Samuel Hopkins Adams
Sarah Bernhardt
Sarah C. Hallowell
Selma Lagerlof
Sherwood Anderson
Sigmund Freud
Standish O'Grady
Stanley Weyman
Stella Benson
Stella M. Francis

Stephen Crane
Stewart Edward White
Stijn Streuvels
Swami Abhedananda
Swami Parmananda
T. S. Ackland
T. S. Arthur
The Princess Der Ling
Thomas A. Janvier
Thomas A Kempis
Thomas Anderton
Thomas Bailey Aldrich
Thomas Bulfinch
Thomas De Quincey
Thomas Dixon
Thomas H. Huxley
Thomas Hardy
Thomas More
Thornton W. Burgess
U. S. Grant
Upton Sinclair
Valentine Williams
Various Authors
Vaughan Kester
Victor Appleton
Victor G. Durham
Victoria Cross
Virginia Woolf
Wadsworth Camp
Walter Camp
Walter Scott
Washington Irving
Wilbur Lawton
Wilkie Collins
Willa Cather
Willard F. Baker
William Dean Howells
William le Queux
W. Makepeace Thackeray
William W. Walter
William Shakespeare
Winston Churchill
Yei Theodora Ozaki
Yogi Ramacharaka
Young E. Allison
Zane Grey